Summer Bridge™

EXPLORATIONS

2-3

CARSON-DELLOSA™
PUBLISHING GROUP

Greensboro, NC 27425 USA

Caution: Exercise activities may require adult supervision. Before beginning any exercise activity, consult a physician. Written parental permission is suggested for those using this book in group situations. Children should always warm up prior to beginning any exercise activity and should stop immediately if they feel any discomfort during exercise.

Caution: Before beginning any food activity, ask parents' permission and inquire about the child's food allergies and religious or other food restrictions.

Caution: Nature activities may require adult supervision. Before beginning any nature activity, ask parents' permission and inquire about the child's plant and animal allergies. Remind the child not to touch plants or animals during the activity without adult supervision.

The authors and publisher are not responsible or liable for any injury that may result from performing the exercises or activities in this book.

Summer Bridge™
An imprint of Carson-Dellosa Publishing LLC
PO Box 35665
Greensboro, NC 27425 USA
carsondellosa.com

ISBN 978-1-4838-1316-5

01-117151151

Table of Contents

Table of Contents (continued)

About Summer Bridge™ Explorations

Summer Bridge™ Explorations includes a variety of resources to prevent learning loss and keep your child thinking, doing, and creating throughout the summer. Practice pages review skills your child learned in kindergarten and preview first grade skills. Throughout, you'll find instructions for completing real-world explorations that encourage your child to actively explore the outdoors, use imagination, and apply skills. Find these resources inside:

- **Three sections that correspond to the three months of a traditional summer vacation**
  Each section begins with an introduction that describes the monthly theme and explains the two real-world explorations your child can choose to complete.

- **Real-world explorations**
  Six hands-on projects connect real-life learning with summer fun. Your child will keep learning alive by applying new skills as he explores the world, close to home and on the road. Look for these symbols beside step-by-step instructions for completing each exploration.

 Exercise Enthusiasts   Dance to the Rhythm

 Take a Trip   Someone Else's Shoes

 Guide to Summer Fun   The Game of Summer

- **Learning activity pages**
  Age-appropriate activities include phonics, writing, counting, addition and subtraction, telling time, learning about shapes, and more. Activities become progressively more challenging as the summer continues. Each month, help your child choose practice pages to build skills and support explorations.

- **Character development and fitness activities**
  Throughout each section, quick activities offer fun ways to think about values, exercise the body, and build strength and fitness inside and out.

- **Bonus science experiments, social studies exercises, and outdoor learning experiences**
  These fun and creative activities are found in each section. Encourage your child to complete them as time allows.

- **Answer key**
  An answer key at the back of the book helps your child check their work.

Fitness and Character Development

Throughout *Summer Bridge™ Explorations*, you and your child will find fun and easy ways to build strong character and a healthy body. These activities encourage your child to think about values and to get fit by focusing on three essential components.

Flexibility

Using and stretching the muscles and joints regularly allows us to accomplish everyday tasks easily, like bending to tie a shoe. Challenge your child to set a stretching goal for the summer, such as practicing daily until he can touch his toes.

It is also important to be mentally flexible. Talk with your child about how disappointing it can be when things don't go your way. Explain that by being flexible, we can choose how we react to circumstances and "make lemonade" when life gives us lemons. Respecting the differences of others, sharing, and taking turns are all ways for your child to practice mental flexibility.

Strength

Your child may think that only people who can lift heavy weights are strong. Explain to your child that she is strong, too. Point out how much stronger she has become since she was a toddler. Many summer activities build strength, such as carrying luggage, riding a bike, swimming, and playing outdoor games.

Inner strength allows us to stand up for what we believe, even when others do not agree. Your child can develop this important character trait by being honest, helping others, and putting her best efforts into every task.

Endurance

Aerobic exercise strengthens the heart and helps blood cells deliver oxygen to the body more efficiently. This summer, limit screen time for your child and encourage him to build endurance by jumping rope, playing tag, hiking, or playing basketball.

Having mental endurance means sticking with something, even if it is difficult. Look for times when your child is growing frustrated or bored with an activity this summer. He may be reluctant to continue swim lessons, baseball practice, or reading a longer book. Whatever it is, encourage him to stay with the task in order to reap the rewards.

Index of Skills

Encouraging Summer Reading

Literacy is the single most important skill that your child needs to be successful in school. The following list includes ideas for ways that you can help your child discover the great adventures of reading!

- Establish a time for reading each day. Ask your child about what she is reading. Try to relate the material to a summer event or to another book.

- Let your child see you reading for enjoyment. Talk about the great things that you discover when you read.

- Choose books from the reading list (pages ix–x), or head to the library and explore. To select a book, have your child read a page aloud.If he does not know more than five of the words, the book may be too difficult.

- Read newspaper and magazine articles, recipes, menus, maps, and street signs on a daily basis to show your child the importance of reading informational texts.

- After you read a fiction book, ask your child to describe the main character to you. How does he or she look or behave? Present your child with several situations. Have her act out how the character would react to those situations.

- Choose several different types of books from the reading list. Talk about genres of books, like folktales, fairy tales, biographies, historical fiction, and informational texts. How many examples can you find from the reading list? Ask your child if he has a favorite type of book. Have your child paint a picture or create a collage that illustrates a book from his favorite genre.

- Make up stories or retell familiar stories. This is especially fun to do in the car, on camping trips, or while waiting at the airport. You can also have your child start a story and let other family members build on it.

- Find the author and illustrator names on the cover of a book and talk about what authors and illustrators do. Ask your child to use the illustrations to tell you about the story.

- Choose a nonfiction book from the reading list or the library. Before you begin reading, ask your child a question about the text. When you finish the book, ask her to write the answer to your question on a piece of paper. If she likes, she can add a drawing to illustrate it.

Summer Reading List

Fiction

Blume, Judy
The Pain and the Great One

Bunting, Eve
So Far From the Sea

Burns, Marilyn
Spaghetti and Meatballs for All!

Cherry, Lynne
*The Great Kapok Tree: A Tale of the
    Amazon Rain Forest*

Cleary, Beverly
Ramona the Pest

Curtis, Gavin
The Bat Boy and His Violin

DeGross, Monalisa
Donovan's Word Jar

dePaola, Tomie
The Art Lesson

Egan, Tim
Dodsworth in Tokyo

Estes, Eleanor
The Hundred Dresses

Falwell, Cathryn
Word Wizard

Henkes, Kevin
The Year of Billy Miller

Holub, Joan
Little Red Writing

Hopkinson, Deborah
Sweet Clara and the Freedom Quilt

Keats, Ezra Jack
Peter's Chair

MacLachlan, Patricia
All the Places to Love

Palatini, Margie
Bedhead
Sweet Tooth

Parish, Peggy
Amelia Bedelia

Pilkey, Dav
Dog Breath

Polacco, Patricia
Mr. Wayne's Masterpiece
Thunder Cake

Rylant, Cynthia
An Angel for Solomon Singer

Say, Allen
Grandfather's Journey

Schotter, Roni
Nothing Ever Happens on 90th Street

Scieszka, Jon
Math Curse
The True Story of the Three Little Pigs

Seuss, Dr.
The Lorax

Silverstein, Shel
A Light in the Attic

Steig, William
Brave Irene

Storad, Conrad J.
Lizards for Lunch: A Roadrunner's Tale

Summer Reading List (continued)

Uchida, Yoshiko
The Bracelet

Van Allsburg, Chris
The Polar Express

Waber, Bernard
Lyle, Lyle, Crocodile

Williams, Margery
The Velveteen Rabbit

Wisniewski, David
The Secret Knowledge of Grown-Ups

Yee, Herbert Wong
A Brand-New Day With Mouse and Mole

Nonfiction

Anno, Masaichiro and Mitsumasa
Anno's Mysterious Multiplying Jar

Berne, Jennifer
On a Beam of Light: A Story of Albert Einstein

Carle, Eric
The Tiny Seed

Christian, Peggy
If You Find a Rock

Dobson, David
Can We Save Them? Endangered Species of North America

Ferrer, J.J.
The Art of Stone Skipping and Other Fun Old-Time Games

George, Jean Craighead
The Tarantula in My Purse and 172 Other Wild Pets

Gibbons, Gail
Nature's Green Umbrella

Hopkinson, Deborah
Anne and Helen

Lester, Helen
Author: A True Story

Llewellyn, Claire
The Best Book of Bugs

Locker, Thomas
Water Dance

Martin, Jacqueline Briggs
Farmer Will Allen and the Growing Table

Mizielinska, Aleksandra and Daniel
Maps

Murphy, Liz
A Dictionary of Dance

Rockwell, Lizzy
The Busy Body Book: A Kid's Guide to Fitness

Rosenstock, Barb
Thomas Jefferson Builds a Library

Schwartz, David M.
How Much Is a Million?

Spelman, Lucy
National Geographic Animal Encyclopedia

Vernick, Audrey
Brothers at Bat: The True Story of an Amazing All-Brother Baseball Team

Section I Introduction

Theme: Learning in the Neighborhood

This month's explorations can be done close to home. They encourage your child to plan and carry out learning experiences both at home and in the neighborhood. Summer, with its more relaxed pace, is a great time for your child to explore the world nearby. Whether searching for insects in the backyard or at the park, attending a farmers' market or community festival, or taking a walk around the block, you will find many opportunities to help your child observe and learn.

To build language arts, reading, and writing skills this month, direct your child toward books or websites where she can learn more about her neighborhood. Suggest that she create a neighborhood guidebook or map that includes details about her favorite places and information on local landmarks. Or, she may like to write a neighborhood newsletter, prepare menus for a special picnic or barbecue, or brainstorm directions for a new game to play outside with friends.

To build math skills this month, look for ways to review time, money, and measurement basics while you are out and about with your child. For example, ask her to use a watch and keep track of how long it takes to drive to the grocery store. Compare weights and unit sizes in the canned-food aisle. After you check out, let her help you count the change. And once you're home, encourage her to create a chart that shows the different types of food and beverages you purchased.

Explorations

This month, your child will have a choice of two explorations. He may choose to follow steps for one or both. Review the explorations below with your child and help him make a choice. Emphasize that it is useful to have a path in mind from the start. Then, help your child find and complete the project activities according to his plan. Throughout the section, your child will see the icons shown below on pages that include directions directly related to one of the explorations. Emphasize that breaking a large project into smaller steps helps make it fun and easy to do.

 **Exercise Enthusiasts**

With this exploration, your child will develop math, communication, and fitness skills by keeping an exercise log, helping friends and family track their exercise habits, and creating a weekly exercise calendar for the summer. Your child's math skills will get a workout as she tracks and organizes data using logs, charts, graphs, and calendars. She will learn to think creatively about exercise as she weighs which activities she does and enjoys most. Finally, her communication skills will be tested by the project's emphasis on getting others involved in building healthy exercise habits.

You can help your child with this exploration by encouraging and motivating her to stick with tracking her exercise. Give safety guidance, involve your child in your own exercise routines, and encourage her to try new activities and sports along the way. Since this project emphasizes involving friends and family in exercise tracking, fill out your own log so your child can make an exercise calendar for you, too.

Dance to the Rhythm

With this exploration, your child will develop math, creative thinking, writing, and fitness skills as he choreographs a tap dance routine and performs it for friends and family. Tap dancing's focus on rhythms, steps, and patterns will help sharpen your child's math skills. The process of choosing a song, choreographing a dance, and designing a routine will require creative thinking. Writing skills will come into play when your child designs a program to inform the audience about his dance. And fitness skills will be honed as your child gets on his feet and starts dancing!

You can help your child with this exploration by being an enthusiastic audience for his rehearsal. In addition, you can offer guidance by suggesting safe spots for him to practice tapping and by helping him come up with appropriate places and times for his performance. On the big day, help him transport and set up any electronic equipment he needs, and offer to help record the performance.

Learning Activities

Practice pages for this month review skills your child learned in second grade. They also focus on skills that support the explorations described above. Preview the activities and choose several that target skills your child needs to practice. Also select several relating to the exploration(s) your child plans to complete. You may wish to mark those pages with a star or other symbol to let her know to begin with those. Then, let your child choose practice activities that interest her and allow her to demonstrate her growing skills.

Exercise Enthusiasts, Step I

Summer is a great time to get outdoors and exercise. This month, design an exercise routine for yourself, and spread the fun by designing routines for your friends and family members, too!

To design an exercise routine for yourself, start by making a chart that shows the kinds of exercise you get. Do you like to run, swim, play tag, jump rope, shoot baskets, or hike? Do you mow the lawn or carry groceries up the stairs? Keep track of everything you do and how often you do it. Each time you do an activity or exercise, check it off on your chart.

Amy's Exercises

Basketball	✔✔✔✔✔✔✔✔✔
Jump rope	✔✔✔✔✔✔✔✔✔✔✔
Jogging	✔✔✔
Soccer	✔
Tag	✔✔✔✔✔
Swimming	✔✔✔
Lawn mowing	✔
Hiking	
Softball	✔
Volleyball	✔✔

After you make a chart for yourself, talk to your friends and family members. Are any of them looking to get more exercise or keep better track of it? Talk to them about the kinds of exercise they get most. Then, make charts for them, too.

Ask them to keep track of their exercise the same way you are. Maybe they would even like to join you when you exercise!

Don't worry if not everyone you ask is able to fill out a chart. Some people won't want to or won't have time, and that's OK. Your goal is just to have fun and spread exercise enthusiasm!

The Synonym Song

Read the song.

Sometimes I talk, but other times I…

shout, whisper, yell, discuss, chatter, or gab.

Sometimes I walk, but other times I…

saunter, tromp, march, step, stroll, trudge, or trek.

Sometimes I run, but other times I…

skip, dash, flee, race, scramble, or scurry.

Sometimes I jump, but other times I…

leap, hop, spring, bound, or vault.

Sometimes I laugh, but other times I…

giggle, chuckle, titter, cackle, or snicker.

Sometimes I sleep, but other times I…

slumber, rest, doze, nap, or snooze.

Use the song to answer the questions.

1. What is a synonym?
   A. a word that means the opposite of another word
   B. a word that sounds like another word but has a different meaning
   C. a word that means the same as another word

2. Draw a line between the synonyms.

talk	leap
walk	snooze
run	giggle
jump	chatter
laugh	stroll
sleep	dash

Circle the word in parentheses that would fit best in each sentence.

3. I will (whisper / shout) a secret in your ear.
4. I will (saunter / march) to the rhythm of the drum.
5. I will (skip / dash) to get some help.
6. I will (cry / laugh) during the funny movie.
7. I will (slumber / nap) all night.
8. I (chuckled / cackled) at the comic in the newspaper.

A thesaurus is a book that lists synonyms of words. You can use a thesaurus to make your writing more interesting. Look at this page from a thesaurus. Then, answer the questions below.

sad (adj): unhappy, down, dismal, morose, miserable, cheerless, gloomy, forlorn, dejected, glum, depressed

said (v): spoke, yelled, whispered, echoed, bellowed, whined, shouted, told, mentioned

9. What does the (adj) after the word *sad* tell you?

_____

10. Rewrite this sentence using a synonym for the word *sad*. **The boy was feeling sad because he lost his puppy.**

_____
_____

Write how many thousands, hundreds, tens, and ones. Then, write the total.

1.
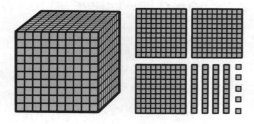

_____ thousand(s) _____ hundred(s)

_____ ten(s) _____ one(s) = _____

2.
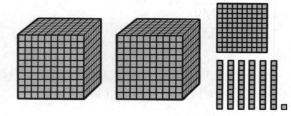

_____ thousand(s) _____ hundred(s)

_____ ten(s) _____ one(s) = _____

3.
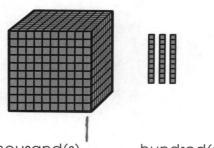

_____ thousand(s) _____ hundred(s)

_____ ten(s) _____ one(s) = _____

4.
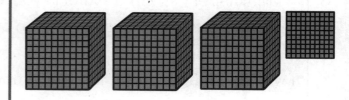

_____ thousand(s) _____ hundred(s)

_____ ten(s) _____ one(s) = _____

5.
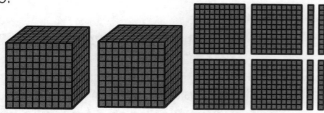

_____ thousand(s) _____ hundred(s)

_____ ten(s) _____ one(s) = _____

6.
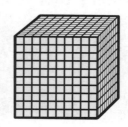
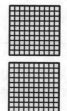

_____ thousand(s) _____ hundred(s)

_____ ten(s) _____ one(s) = _____

Combine each pair of sentences using the conjunction in parentheses ( ). In each new sentence, place a comma before the conjunction.

EXAMPLE: My grandma raises bees. She has only been stung once. (but)
My grandma raises bees, but she has only been stung once.

1.   Liam wanted to bike to the park. He got a flat tire. (but)

_____

2.   Keisha is moving to Idaho. Her family hasn't found a house yet. (but)

_____

3.   The fireworks lit up the night sky. Everyone cheered. (so)

_____

4.   Mr. Gomez coaches our softball team. I think he does a great job. (and)

_____

Read each word aloud. Listen to the vowel sounds. If the word has a short vowel sound, write _S_ on the line. If the word has a long vowel sound, write _L_ on the line.

EXAMPLE:

rust   **S**   5.   face _____   6.   clock _____

7.   cute _____   8.   big _____   9.   shut _____

10.   bike _____   11.   apple _____   12.   boat _____

13.   road _____   14.   yell _____   15.   read _____

Write each number in expanded form.

		Thousands	Hundreds	Tens	Ones
1.	9,516 =		+	+	+
2.	2,358 =		+	+	+
3.	1,407 =		+	+	+
4.	921 =		+	+	+
5.	7,800 =		+	+	+
6.	3,264 =		+	+	+
7.	5,182 =		+	+	+
8.	614 =		+	+	+
9.	4,073 =		+	+	+
10.	9,530 =		+	+	+

FITNESS FLASH: Stand up straight with a chair right behind you. Stretch your arms straight in front of you and slowly sit. Stop right before your bottom touches the chair and slowly stand up again. Repeat this 10 times.

Add to solve each problem.

1. 9	2. 2	3. 0	4. 8	5. 5
+ 7	+ 3	+ 2	+ 3	+ 2

6. 4	7. 17	8. 8	9. 3	10. 2
+ 4	+ 1	+ 4	+ 1	+ 7

11. 1	12. 6	13. 6	14. 5	15. 15
+ 2	+ 2	+ 7	+ 9	+ 3

Subtract to solve each problem.

16. 4	17. 12	18. 6	19. 9	20. 13
− 2	− 7	− 4	− 4	− 5

21. 11	22. 19	23. 9	24. 3	25. 17
− 4	− 6	− 6	− 3	− 7

26. 17	27. 7	28. 3	29. 20	30. 12
− 8	− 5	− 0	− 3	− 4

FACTOID: Honeybees communicate with each other by dancing.

9

Aunt Antonym

Read the story.

We have a nickname for my mother's sister. We call her Aunt Antonym. She always says or does the opposite of what we say or do. At the zoo, we began at the north end of the park. My aunt began at the south end. At the monkey cage, we thought the monkeys were adorable. My aunt thought they were ugly. I said a zebra is a white horse with black stripes. My aunt said a zebra is a black horse with white stripes. At the dolphin show, we sat in the front. We like getting wet. My aunt sat in the back. She wanted to stay dry. Soon, we were hungry. My aunt was still full from breakfast. After lunch, we rode the train around the zoo. My aunt wanted to walk. Finally, my aunt said she was ready to go. We wished we could have stayed.

10

Use the story to answer the questions.

1. Write *T* before the statements that are true and *F* before the statements that are false.

    _____ The author is writing about his sister.

    _____ Aunt Antonym is the real name of the author's aunt.

    _____ Aunt Antonym thinks monkeys are ugly.

    _____ Aunt Antonym wanted to sit in the back at the dolphin show because she didn't like to get wet.

2. Why did the author call his aunt Aunt Antonym?

    _____

    _____

    _____

3. An antonym is a word that means the opposite of another word. For example, an antonym of *big* is *little*. Write a word from the story that is an antonym for each word below.

    north _____   ugly _____

    black _____   front_____

    dry _____   hungry _____

    stay_____   brother _____

4. Write the past tense for each verb.

    begin _____   think _____

    say _____   ride _____

    sit _____   is _____

    have _____   wish _____

You have discovered a hidden treasure! Round the value in each treasure chest to the nearest hundred. The first one is done for you.

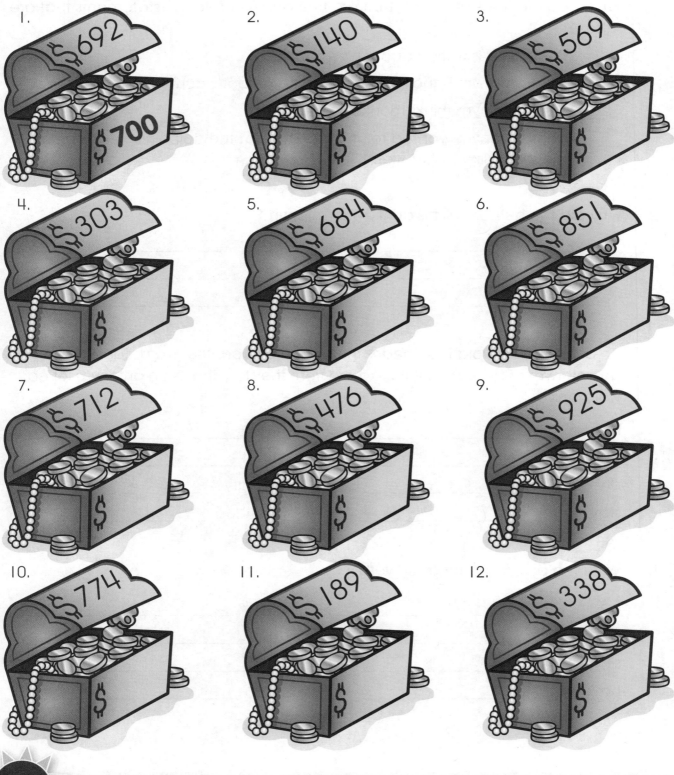

1. $692 $700

2. $140

3. $569

4. $303

5. $684

6. $851

7. $712

8. $476

9. $925

10. $774

11. $189

12. $338

Count by 2. Write the missing numbers.

1.

   2,   4,   6,   _____,   10,   12,   _____

2. 16, _____, _____, 22, 24, _____, 28, 30, 32

Count by 5. Write the missing numbers.

3.

   5,   10,   _____, _____,   25,   _____, _____

4. 20, _____, 30, _____, _____, 45, 50, 55, _____, 65

   _____, 75, _____, _____, 90

Count by 10. Write the missing numbers.

5. _____   _____   _____

Count backward by 10. Write the missing numbers.

6. 100, 90, _____, 70, _____, 50, _____, _____, 20, 10

Read each word aloud. Then, write *short* or *long* for each vowel sound.

1. bug _____
2. cake _____
3. jut _____
4. hum _____
5. road _____
6. catch _____
7. cube _____
8. lock _____
9. sick _____
10. mild _____
11. mop _____
12. these _____
13. street _____
14. log _____
15. spy _____
16. goat _____

Words that name holidays, places, and products are proper nouns. Underline the proper noun or nouns in each sentence.

17. Have you ever been to Portland, Oregon?

18. Let's make cards for Valentine's Day.

19. My grandmother lives in Japan.

20. We always buy Papa Louie's pizza when we have family movie night.

21. Our neighbors moved here from Chicago, Illinois.

22. I'd like a glass of orange juice and a bowl of Crunch Os for breakfast.

23. Are you going to wear green on St. Patrick's Day?

Circle the numeral that is the least.

1.	173	149	156	206	347	165
2.	699	943	943	878	566	903
3.	510	430	530	770	680	820
4.	390	745	845	691	759	425
5.	941	812	852	814	916	804

Circle the numeral that is the greatest.

6.	746	981	873	699	870	847
7.	633	709	599	671	433	598
8.	695	768	845	871	555	796
9.	493	561	664	793	990	889
10.	567	765	675	783	623	805

Use greater than (>) and less than (<) signs to compare numerals.

11.	439 _____ 670	944 _____ 872	730 _____ 750
12.	610 _____ 603	567 _____ 576	887 _____ 891
13.	991 _____ 919	499 _____ 500	635 _____ 471
14.	781 _____ 902	1000 _____ 998	549 _____ 798
15.	473 _____ 374	895 _____ 958	768 _____ 391
16.	399 _____ 405	818 _____ 881	914 _____ 941

Dance to the Rhythm, Step I

In this exploration, you will make tap shoes and then make up a dance to a favorite song. You will add rhythms that fit with the music, memorize the choreography, and practice with a friend. When it's ready, perform your dance for friends and family!

First, make your tap shoes.

What you'll need:
- A pair of shoes with a relatively smooth sole (avoid shoes with thick traction).
- 2 pieces of elastic—8 inches long and ½ inch wide
- 2 large metal washers—1¾ inch in diameter

What to do:
1. Put on your shoes

2. For each shoe, thread the elastic through the washer. Wrap it around your shoe so the washer is under the ball of your foot. Make sure the washer lies flat against your shoe.

3. Pull the elastic tight and make a knot on top of your shoe. You want the elastic to be tight enough that it doesn't fall off but not so tight that you can't pull it off later.

Now, try making different kinds of sounds with your shoes. Ask an adult to help you find a floor or hard surface that's safe to practice on.

Making a Compass

A compass is a magnet that can identify geographic direction. It is very easy and a lot of fun to make your own compass!

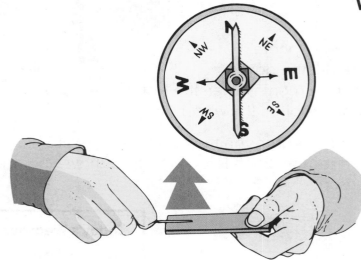

What you'll need:
- magnet
- steel sewing needle
- piece of thin plastic foam (from fast-food packaging)
- shallow glass or plastic bowl
- masking tape
- water

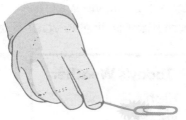

What to do:

1. Pull the sewing needle towards you across the magnet. Repeat this 20 times. Be sure to always pull in the same direction.

2. Test your needle on a steel object. If it is not yet magnetized, repeat step #1.

3. Tape the needle to a small piece of plastic foam.

4. Float your magnet in a dish of water.

What happened?
Wait for your floating needle to stop spinning. In what direction is it pointing?

_____

Try giving the float needle a spin. Wait for it to stop spinning.

Now, what direction is it pointing? _____

BONUS

Leaning Into Summer

Why isn't it summer all year long? The seasons change because Earth is tilted like the Leaning Tower of Pisa. As Earth orbits the sun, it stays tilting in the same direction in space.

Let's look at the seasons in the Northern Hemisphere. When the North Pole is tilting toward the sun, the days become warmer and longer. It is summer. Six months later, the North Pole tilts away from the sun. The days become cooler and shorter. It is winter.

Directions: Label the Northern Hemisphere's seasons on the chart below. Write a make-believe weather forecast for each season. Each forecast should show what the weather is like in your region for that season.

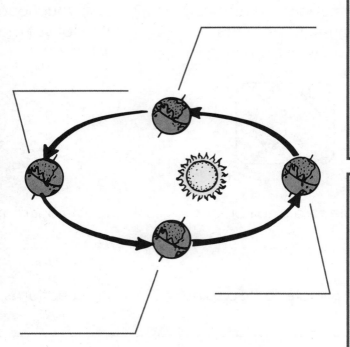

Today's Weather

High _____ Low _____

Sunrise _____

Sunset _____

Forecast

_____

_____

_____

_____

Today's Weather

High _____ Low _____

Sunrise _____

Sunset _____

Forecast

_____

_____

_____

_____

Today's Weather

High _____ Low _____

Sunrise _____

Sunset _____

Forecast

_____

_____

_____

_____

Today's Weather

High _____ Low _____

Sunrise _____

Sunset _____

Forecast

_____

_____

_____

_____

Look at each word. Write how many vowels you see. Then, read each word aloud.
Write how many vowel sounds you hear.

		Vowels	Vowel Sounds			Vowels	Vowel Sounds
1.	muzzle	_____	_____	9.	radio	_____	_____
2.	cookies	_____	_____	10.	merit	_____	_____
3.	socks	_____	_____	11.	deep	_____	_____
4.	alphabet	_____	_____	12.	wanted	_____	_____
5.	oak	_____	_____	13.	heart	_____	_____
6.	junk	_____	_____	14.	useful	_____	_____
7.	pilot	_____	_____	15.	beautiful	_____	_____
8.	melting	_____	_____	16.	otter	_____	_____

**Think about your favorite food. Describe this food using each of your five senses.
What do you see, hear, feel, smell, and taste?**

_____

_____

_____

_____

_____

_____

Add or subtract to solve each problem.

1. There are 13 bananas.

   Kit takes 5.

   How many bananas are left? _____

2. The Nowaks have 6 apples.

   Mrs. Nowak buys 5 more.

   How many apples do they have now? _____

3. The store has 11 boxes of plums.

   4 boxes of plums are sold.

   How many boxes are left? _____

4. Together, Holly and her sister bought 18 bananas.

   Holly bought 8 bananas.

   8 + _____ 🍌 = 18

   How many bananas did her sister buy? _____

5. Mrs. Chang has 17 hats.

   3 of the hats have bows.

   How many hats do not have bows? _____

Yvette asked her classmates about their pets. She made this bar graph to show the results.

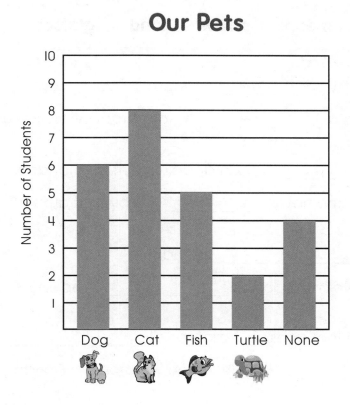

Our Pets

Use the bar graph to answer the questions.

1. Which pet do the most students have? _____

2. How many students have a dog or a cat? _____

3. How many students have pets? _____

4. How many students did Yvette talk to? _____

5. How many students have either a fish or a turtle? _____

Write the homonym from the word bank that makes sense with the context clues in each pair of sentences.

tire	break	mean	straw	land	glasses	book	free

1. Be careful not to _____ Mom's favorite vase.

    Should we take a _____ from practice to eat lunch?

2. Mom will _____ an appointment for Monday.

    Have you read the new _____ by that author?

3. What do you _____ by that?

    The dog that lives next door is _____, so let's stay away.

4. My cat is so old that chasing a mouse will _____ her out.

    We got a flat _____ when we drove to Florida.

5. The plane is due to _____ at 6:00 tonight.

    The large areas of _____ on Earth are called continents.

6. The zookeeper lifted the door to _____ the bird.

    I can't believe we read enough books to earn _____ pizza!

7. After you finish, set your lemonade _____ on the counter.

    I am going to get new _____ to help me see the board.

8. The farmer keeps _____ in the barn during the winter.

    Can you hand me a _____ for my milk shake?

Color the number boxes to show skip counting.

1. Start at 0 and count by fours.

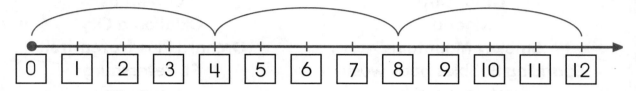

2. Start at 0 and count by sixes.

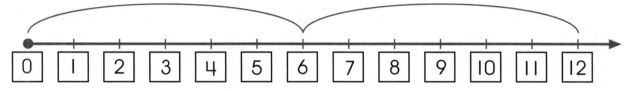

3. Start at 33 and count by threes.

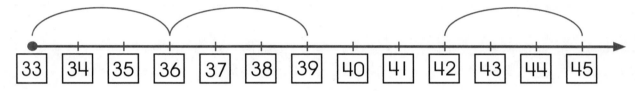

4. Start at 62 and count by twos.

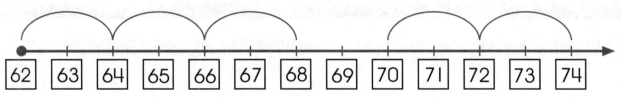

5. Start at 84 and count by fours.

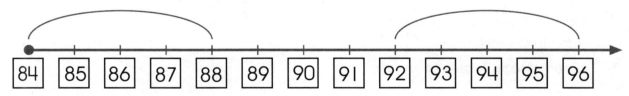

CHARACTER CHECK: Think of three friends or family members who have helped you recently. Tell them "Thank you!"

Write each proper noun from the word bank in the correct column.

Labor Day	Christmas
Nigeria	Oklahoma City
Smokey Mountains	Orchard Plus frozen fruit
Sparkling Bubbles body wash	St. Petersburg
Aunt Jane's pies	Kwanzaa

Holidays	Products	Places
_____	_____	_____
_____	_____	_____
_____	_____	_____
_____	_____	_____

Circle the adverb in each sentence. Then, underline the verb each adverb modifies.

1. The dogs barked loudly at the sound of the vacuum cleaner.

2. I looked everywhere for my mitten.

3. Nadia swims faster than I do.

4. Gerardo walked slowly down the sidewalk.

5. Wynona awoke early on Sunday morning.

6. Let's play outside in the backyard.

Measurement

Write the length of each object in inches.

1.

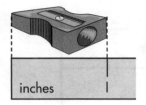

_____ inches

2.

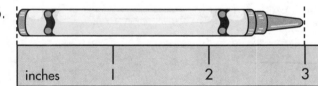

_____ inch

3.

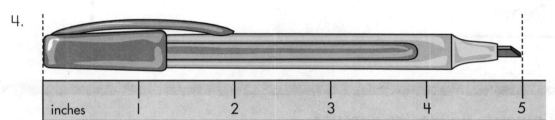

_____ inches

4.

_____ inches

5.

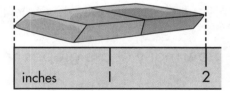

_____ inches

6.

_____ inches

7.

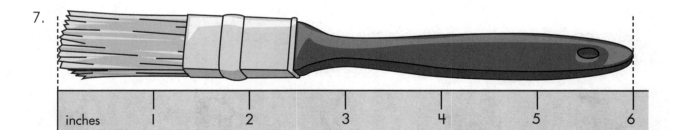

_____ inches

Dylan polled his classmates about their favorite fruits. He made this picture graph with the results. One piece of fruit on the graph means one person.

Our Favorite Fruits

Apples	🍎 🍎 🍎
Oranges	🍊 🍊 🍊 🍊 🍊
Bananas	🍌 🍌 🍌 🍌
Grapes	🍇 🍇 🍇
Pears	🍐 🍐 🍐

Use the picture graph to answer the questions.

1. How many classmates chose either bananas or oranges? _____

2. How many classmates told Dylan their favorite fruit? _____

3. How many chose grapes or pears? _____

4. How many classmates did not choose oranges? _____

5. Which fruit did the most classmates choose? _____

6. How many more chose bananas than chose grapes? _____

When a prefix is added to a base word, it changes the meaning of the word. Circle the prefix in each word. Then, write the letter of the correct definition next to the word.

1. _____ reuse
2. _____ unhappy
3. _____ misstep
4. _____ unfrozen
5. _____ misread

A. to wrongly step
B. not happy
C. to wrongly read
D. to use again
E. not frozen

When a suffix is added to a base word, it changes the meaning of the word. Add -less or -ness to the base word in each sentence.
EXAMPLE:

The students were very _____ rest **less** _____ today.

6. The ____ silli ____ of the clowns made us giggle.

7. Trying to train my dog to fetch is ____ hope ____.

8. The baby loves the ____ fuzzi ____ of her stuffed bear.

9. The ____ loud ____ of the noise made me jump.

10. Her ____ sad ____ showed on her face.

Exercise Enthusiasts, Step 2

Now, it's time to find out which exercises you are doing the most. Organize the information you have been collecting into a graph.

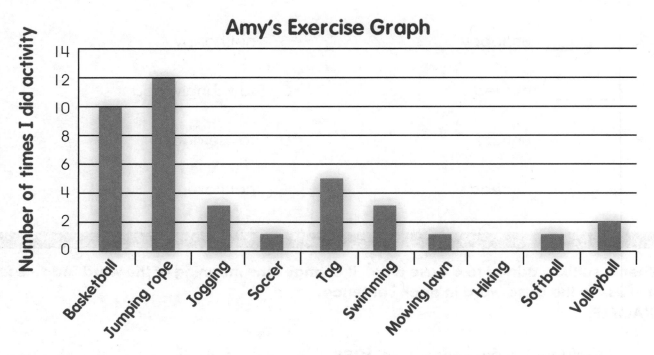

Are there any exercise you haven't been doing often or don't like doing? Decide whether you need to focus more on those exercises or take them out of your routine.

Also, are there any exercises you would like to start doing? Add them to the chart you made in Step 1.

After you make a graph for your own exercise routine, talk to the friends and family members you made charts for. Make graphs for them. Find out what they would like to add to their exercise routines and what they would like to subtract.

Scales, Feathers, Hair

Directions:
Before this activity, collect pictures of animals. Write down two or more observations regarding the outside of your animals (for example, the birds are colorful, the puppies are furry, the snakes don't look that slimy, etc.). Share your observations.

Now, categorize your pictures into three groups by looking at what is on the exterior of your animals. How did you decide which animals would be grouped together? On paper, create three columns. Title one "Fish," one "Birds" and one "Mammals" and glue pictures under the specific category listed.

Glue each animal under the proper category. When the supply of pictures has been exhausted, make generalizations about the coverings of animals (for example, if an animal has feathers, it is a bird.) You can judge an animal by its cover!

Take It Outside!

Paper grocery bags make great safari jackets. Cut out holes for your neck and arms. Add a rope belt and some binoculars. Tape on paper pockets to hold your treasures. Grab a map and canteen, and start your adventure quest!

Going on an outside quest is much safer if you know what plants to avoid. Ask an adult to help you look up pictures of poison oak, ivy, and sumac, and stinging nettle. Can you spot any of these plants? Look, but do not touch!

Which way is the wind blowing? Pick up a few pieces of grass and toss them in the air, watching which way they move in the wind. You may have to do this a few times to be sure of the direction.

Write the time two ways. The first one is done for you.

1.

    7 o'clock

    7 : 00

2.

    _____ o'clock

    _____ : _____

3.

    _____ o'clock

    _____ : _____

4.

    _____ o'clock

    _____ : _____

5.

    _____ o'clock

    _____ : _____

6.

    _____ o'clock

    _____ : _____

7.

    _____ o'clock

    _____ : _____

8.

    _____ o'clock

    _____ : _____

9.

    _____ o'clock

    _____ : _____

A Bird's Life

Read the passage below.

Birds are unique animals. Birds have wings, feathers, and beaks. Birds are the only animals that have feathers. Feathers enable most birds to fly. Their ability to fly helps them stay alive because they can hunt for food, escape their enemies, and migrate away from bad weather. Feathers also protect birds from getting too hot or too cold. Birds have beaks, but they do not have teeth. They use their beaks to get food. Birds eat insects, worms, seeds, and grains.

Birds are protective parents. They lay eggs and build nests to protect their eggs. Usually, the mother bird sits on the nest to keep the eggs warm. Both the mother and father bird keep watch over the nest before the eggs hatch. Nests continue to keep baby birds warm after they hatch from their eggs. Adult birds take care of baby birds until they are ready to fly. They bring food to the baby birds in the nest.

Use the passage to answer the questions.

1. Circle the sentence that tells the main idea.

    A. Birds are unique animals.

    B. The adult bird teaches its babies how to fly and find food.

    C. Birds are one of the few animals that lay eggs.

2. Fill in the blanks with the correct answers.

    Birds are the only animals that have
    _____.

    Birds do not have
    _____.

    Birds lay _____.

    Birds build _____ to
    protect their eggs.

3. Number the sentences in the order
    that they happen.

    _____ The adult birds bring food to
    the baby birds in the nest.

    _____ The mother bird sits on the
    nest to keep the eggs warm.

    _____ Birds build a nest to protect
    their eggs.

    _____ The adult birds teach their
    babies how to fly and find food.

4. Write a *T* if the sentence is true. Write
    an *F* if the sentence is false.

    _____ All birds can fly.

    _____ Flying helps birds find food.

    _____ Flying protects birds from their
    enemies.

    _____ Birds migrate to stay away
    from their enemies.

    _____ Some birds have large teeth.

5. What does *migrate* mean?

    A. to hide under trees

    B. to fly to other places

    C. to find shelter

Action verbs tell what the subject of a sentence does. Circle the action verb in each sentence.

6. Birds fly with the help of their feathers.

7. Birds eat with their beaks instead of teeth.

8. Birds build nests for their eggs.

9. Baby birds hatch from eggs.

10. Adult birds bring their baby birds food.

Add to solve each problem.

1.	23 +42	2.	64 +25	3.	47 +34	4.	13 +45	5.	55 +30

6. 70
+29 7. 82
+11 8. 74
+23 9. 58
+41 10. 26
+33

11. 12
+77 12. 83
+13 13. 41
+37 14. 19
+60 15. 22
+37

16. 15
+72 17. 18
+81 18. 84
+12 19. 27
+62 20. 46
+41

21. 52
+36 22. 75
+10 23. 24
+43 24. 51
+27 25. 29
+50

26. 31
+55 27. 47
+32 28. 19
+30 29. 62
+37 30. 33
+52

Use the information in the tally chart to complete the bar graph.

Points in the Basketball Game

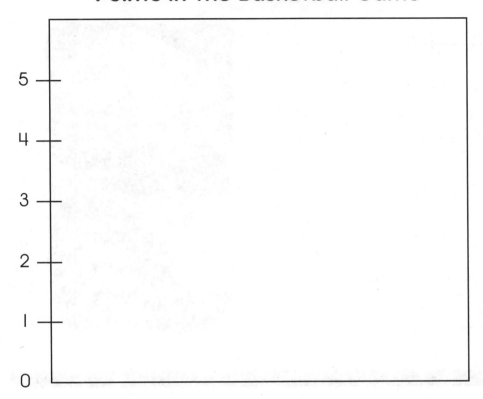

Points in the Basketball Game	
Cara	I I I
Evan	++++
Dawn	I I I I
Hugo	I

Use the bar graph to answer the questions.

1. Which student scored the least points? _____

2. Which student scored the most points? _____

3. How many points were scored altogether in the basketball game? _____

4. How many more points did Evan score than Hugo? _____

Underline the compound word in each sentence. Then, draw a line between the two word parts.
EXAMPLE:

Rashad lives on a <u>house|boat</u>.

1. A snowflake hit the red fox on the nose.

2. Let's go play in the treehouse.

3. Did you hear the doorbell ring?

4. The cows are in the cornfield.

5. I cleaned my bedroom this evening.

6. The raindrops fell very quickly.

Similar words can have different shades of meaning. Underline the word that best completes each sentence.

7. Luis eagerly (sipped, gulped) the cold water when he returned from his bike ride.

8. The glass (shattered, broke) as it hit the floor.

9. "Please don't (gobble, nibble) the grapes so fast!" exclaimed Mom.

10. Samantha was (furious, upset) that her scooter had been stolen.

11. Antoine (pounded, tapped) on the door, hoping he wouldn't wake the baby.

Use "counting on" to find the total value of the coins.

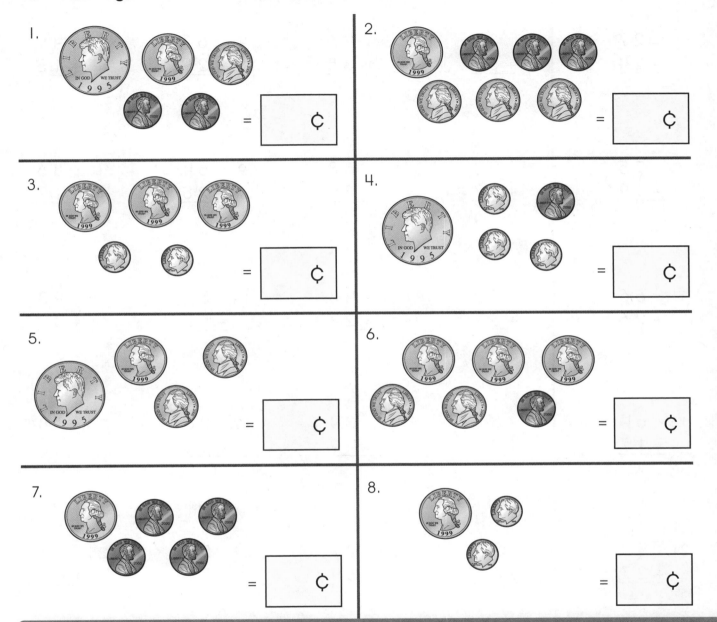

1. _____ = [   ] ¢

2. _____ = [   ] ¢

3. _____ = [   ] ¢

4. _____ = [   ] ¢

5. _____ = [   ] ¢

6. _____ = [   ] ¢

7. _____ = [   ] ¢

8. _____ = [   ] ¢

Good Deed for the Day

Good deeds show thoughtfulness for others, and they make you feel great, too! Look around your neighborhood for good deeds you could do. You could pick up litter, help a neighbor carry in grocery bags, or help someone mow the lawn and pull weeds. Think of a new good deed to do each day this week. You could even get your friends involved and spread the good deeds even further!

Add to solve each problem. Regroup if necessary.

1. 27
   + 24

2. 39
   + 53

3. 46
   + 35

4. 57
   + 29

5. 49
   + 15

6. 75
   + 19

7. 93
   + 37

8. 58
   + 34

9. 64
   + 28

10. 86
   + 17

11. 66
   + 26

12. 79
   + 32

13. 43
   + 27

14. 56
   + 58

15. 98
   + 32

16. 64
   + 17

17. 57
   + 26

18. 34
   + 49

19. 25
   + 36

20. 18
   + 28

21. 43
   + 27

22. 26
   + 36

23. 27
   + 69

24. 53
   + 37

25. 33
   + 48

CHARACTER CHECK: The next time you get angry or upset about something, take a deep breath and count to 10 before you do or say anything about it.

Choose a title to describe the main idea of the entire passage below. Then, choose the topic sentence for each paragraph. Circle your answers.

Lobsters are saltwater animals that belong to a group called *crustaceans*. They have a hard outer shell and five sets of legs. The first set of legs has claws. One claw is usually used for crushing, and the other for biting. The female lobster lays thousands of eggs. The tiny young drift and swim for three to five weeks before settling on the bottom of the ocean.

Crayfish are freshwater cousins of lobsters. Crawfish, as they are also called, may be as short as two inches in length. Like their lobster cousins, crayfish have large front claws that are actually one of five sets of legs. Crayfish are found around the world in freshwater rivers and streams, except in Africa and Antarctica.

1. A good title for this passage would be:

    A. River Animals

    B. Lobsters

    C. Cousins with Claws

2. The topic sentence in the first paragraph is:

    A. The first set of legs has claws.

    B. They have a hard outer shell and five sets of legs.

    C. Lobsters are saltwater animals that belong to a group called *crustaceans*.

3. The topic sentence in the second paragraph is:

    A. Crawfish, as they are also called, may be as short as two inches in length.

    B. Crayfish are freshwater cousins of lobsters.

    C. Crayfish are found in freshwater rivers and streams.

FACTOID: After crayfish shed their old shells, they eat them! This provides the crayfish with much-needed calcium.

Circle the groups that are odd.

Tell how many. Label odd or even. Write an equation. The first one is done for you.

1.  ____**5**____ jets ____**odd**____ ____**3**____ + ____**2**____ = ____**5**____	2.  _____ bears _____ _____ + _____ = _____
3.  _____ dolls _____ _____ + _____ = _____	4.  _____ cars _____ _____ + _____ = _____

Read each sentence. Then, write the letter of the underlined word's definition.
EXAMPLE:

   B   The superhero can <u>fly</u>.   A.   a small winged insect

   A   The frog ate the <u>fly</u>.   B.   to move through the air

1. _____ Please turn on the <u>light</u>.   A.   a lamp

   _____ The backpack is <u>light</u>.   B.   not heavy

2. _____ <u>Store</u> the books in the box.   A.   a place to buy things

   _____ I bought a shirt at the <u>store</u>.   B.   to put away for the future

3. _____ Toss a coin in the <u>well</u>.   A.   healthy

   _____ Are you feeling <u>well</u>?   B.   a hole to access underground water

If you could keep only three of your toys and had to give the rest away, which three toys would you keep? Why?

_____

_____

_____

_____

_____

Exercise Enthusiasts, Step 3

Now that you have focused in on your favorite exercises, it's time to develop your routine even more!

Set goals for each activity you do. If you bicycle, how far do you usually ride? Maybe you can add more miles to your routine. If you play basketball, how often do you shoot free throws? Maybe you can hit the court twice a week instead of once.

Look at the example in the box below. Then, list each of your exercises. List a goal next to each exercise.

Amy's Exercise Goals

Basketball — Goal: shoot 100 free throws every day

Jump rope — Goal: jump for 15 minutes every day

Tag — Goal: play twice a week for 30 minutes

Bicycling — Goal: go on two 5-mile rides every week

Once you have set goals for yourself, talk to the friends and family members you are helping with their exercise routines. Find out what goals they would like to set.

_____

_____

_____

_____

_____

Find the Landmarks

Geographers can tell us how places are the same and how they are different. Where you live is different from where your friend lives. Maybe you live southwest of school while your friend lives north of the school.

Directions: Write the names and draw pictures of landmarks that are found near your school. Place each one one the chart in its correct location relative to your school.

Northwest	North	Northeast
West	School	East
Southwest	South	Southeast

The Life Cycle of a Frog

The frog goes through many changes during its life. Read about the frog's life cycle below. Then, complete the word puzzle using what you have learned.

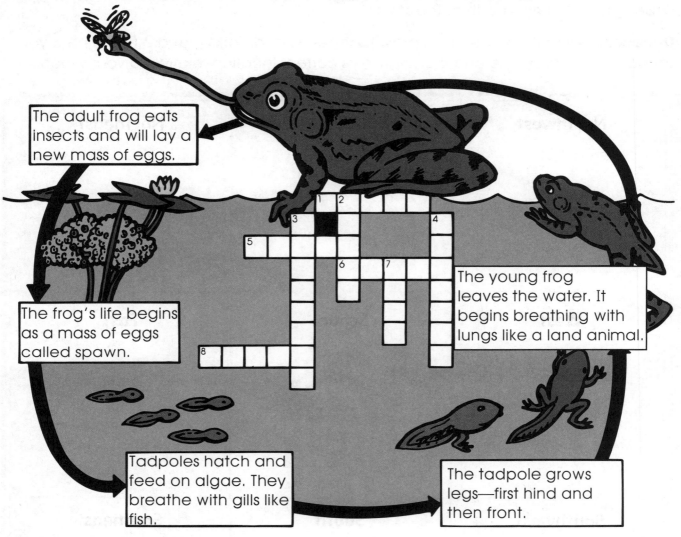

The adult frog eats insects and will lay a new mass of eggs.

The frog's life begins as a mass of eggs called spawn.

The young frog leaves the water. It begins breathing with lungs like a land animal.

Tadpoles hatch and feed on algae. They breathe with gills like fish.

The tadpole grows legs—first hind and then front.

Across:

1. Tadpoles feed on ____.
5. A mass of eggs is called ____.
6. Tadpoles breathe with ____.
8. The frog's changes are called its life ____.

Down:

2. Adult frogs breathe with ____.
3. Eggs hatch into ____.
4. Adult frogs eat ____.
7. Tadpoles grow ____.

Use the information in the tally chart to complete the picture graph.

Shapes Around the Kitchen	
Triangles	
Stars	
Squares	
Circles	

Shapes Around the Kitchen	
▲	☐☐☐☐☐ I
☆	☐☐☐☐☐ ☐☐☐☐☐
■	☐☐☐☐☐ III
●	☐☐☐☐☐

Use the picture graph to answer the questions below.

1. What shape is seen the most around the kitchen? _____

2. How many more squares ■ are there than circles ● ? _____

3. What shape is seen the least around the kitchen? _____

4. How many more stars ☆ are there than triangles ▲ ? _____

Circle each word that has the /ōō/ sound, as in *tooth*. Draw an X on each word that has the /ŏŏ/ sound, as in *hook*.

look	coo	loot	goof	cook
hood	soon	wool	scoop	cool
took	toot	food	brook	crook
mood	wood	moose	book	goose
school	fool	zoo	spoon	nook

Change the spelling of each underlined word to make it plural. Use the word bank if you need help.

Word bank: feet, geese, wolves, lives, oxen, mice, teeth

1. more than one <u>ox</u> _____
2. more than one <u>tooth</u> _____
3. more than one <u>life</u> _____
4. more than one <u>goose</u> _____
5. more than one <u>wolf</u> _____
6. more than one <u>mouse</u> _____
7. more than one <u>foot</u> _____

Subtract to solve each problem.

1. 86
   − 32

2. 52
   − 12

3. 67
   − 45

4. 95
   − 30

5. 87
   − 26

6. 39
   − 13

7. 66
   − 46

8. 38
   − 14

9. 75
   − 52

10. 88
   − 37

11. 47
   − 15

12. 96
   − 73

13. 58
   − 54

14. 81
   − 21

15. 57
   − 33

16. 36
   − 14

17. 87
   − 77

18. 70
   − 30

19. 65
   − 50

20. 99
   − 73

21. 97
   − 25

22. 64
   − 23

23. 72
   − 22

24. 89
   − 55

25. 55
   − 14

FITNESS FLASH: Clap your hands in front of your body as fast as you can for 30 seconds. Then, clap behind your back for 30 seconds. How many times can you clap each way?

Use the information from the chart to find the answers.

Assignment Schedule					
	Reading	**Writing**	**Math**	**Science**	**S. Studies**
Monday	unit 1	brainstorm	p. 21–22	plant seeds	none
Tuesday	unit 2	rough draft	p. 23–24	none	finish map
Wednesday	unit 3	edit	p. 25–26	record growth	none
Thursday	unit 4	revision	p. 27–28	none	time line
Friday	none	final draft	line graph	record growth	none

1. What assignment is due Wednesday in Science? _____

2. What assignment is due Thursday in Writing?_____

3. On what day is the time line due in Social Studies? _____

4. In what subject is the assignment to complete pages 27–28 for Thursday?

    _____

5. What assignment is due Monday in Social Studies? _____

6. On what day is unit 2 due in Reading? _____

7. On what day is the line graph due in Math? _____

8. What assignment is due Tuesday in Writing? _____

9. On what day are no assignments due in two classes? _____

CHARACTER CHECK: Which school subject is hardest for you? What can you do to improve at it during the next school year?

Name each shape.

1.

_____

2.

_____

3.

_____

4.

_____

5.

_____

6.

_____

7.

_____

8.

_____

Circle the shape named. Then, answer the questions.

9. square pyramid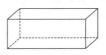

10. cube

11. sphere

12. Which shape has 6 equal faces? _____

13. Which shape is completely round and 3-D? _____

14. Which shape has 2 pairs of equal sides? _____

15. Which shape has 5 total angles? _____

Collective nouns name groups of people, animals, or things. Choose a collective noun from the word bank to complete each sentence.

herd	flock	fleet	bouquet	colony

1. Sasha found a _____ of ants under the rock.

2. A _____ of ships sailed out of the harbor.

3. A _____ of sheep grazed in the meadow.

4. Victor picked a _____ of flowers for Mom's birthday.

5. Maddie saw a _____ of cows gather in the pasture.

A possessive noun in each sentence is missing an apostrophe. Add an apostrophe like this: **Chelsea's kitty.**

1. Thads mask scared his little sister.

2. All of a sudden, the televisions screen went blank.

3. Digbys fur is getting too shaggy.

4. Did you hit the piñata at Marias birthday party?

5. Dads new sweater looks very cozy.

Count 3-digit numbers by 1.

1. Start at 430.

    430, 431, 432, _____, 434, _____, _____, 437

2. Start at 215.

    215, 216, _____, 218, _____, 220, _____, 222

Skip count 3-digit numbers.

3. Count by 5. Start at 500.

    500, 505, _____, _____, _____,525, 530, _____

4. Count by 5. Start at 680.

    680, _____, 690, _____, 700, 705, _____, _____

5. Count by 10. Start at 200.

    200, _____, _____, 230, _____, 250, _____, 270

6. Count by 10. Start at 350.

    350, _____, 370, _____, _____, 400, _____, _____

7. Count by 100. Start at 100.

    100, _____, 300, _____, _____, 600, _____

8. Count backward by 100. Start at 800.

    800, 700, _____, _____, 400, _____, _____

FITNESS FLASH: Walk from your room to your front door. Count how many steps it takes you to get there.

Read the passage. Then, answer the questions.

Birds make nests in many places. Woodpeckers make nests in tree trunks. Crows build them in high branches. A quail digs a shallow hole under a bush for a nest. Some desert owls build nests inside cacti. Swallows build mud nests under bridges. Wherever they live, birds find safe places to raise their babies.

1. Name four places birds can make nests.

   _____   _____

   _____   _____

2. Why do birds make nests?

   _____

   _____

3. Where do woodpeckers build their nests?

   _____

4. What kind of bird builds mud nests under bridges?

   _____

5. What kind of bird builds a nest in a cactus?

   _____

6. Where do quails build their nests?

   _____

FITNESS FLASH: Do 10 jumping jacks. Clap your hands above your head each time.

Dance to the Rhythm, Step 2

It's time to make sounds with your shoes—and make up a dance to one of your favorite songs!

See what happens when you step, lightly tap, or slide your foot along the floor. What does it sound like if you jump with both feet? How fast can you tap? What rhythms can you make by combining different movements?

Try the patterns below, or make up some of your own. Take turns tapping out patterns with a friend. Then, see what happens when the two of you tap out two different patterns at the same time.

- Step Tap Tap, Step Tap Tap
- Step Tap Slide, Step Tap Slide
- Slide Slide Tap Step, Slide Slide Tap Step
- Jump Tap, Slide Tap, Step Tap Tap
- Jump Tap Tap Tap, Step Tap Tap Tap

Now, listen to some of your favorite songs. Are they fast or slow? Pop, country, rap, or rock? Try out some tap moves to each song. See how many different rhythms fit with each one. Then, answer the questions below.

1. How many different tap rhythms did you use in each song? To which song did you dance the most rhythms?

   _____

   _____

2. Did any of the songs inspire you to create new tap rhythms or moves? If so, which ones?

   _____

   _____

3. Which song was the easiest to tap dance to?

   _____

4. Choose the song you want to use for your dance and write the artist and title here:

   _____

Dance to the Rhythm, Step 2

Listen to your song over and over. Pay close attention to the rhythms and tap along with your fingers and toes. Write down notes about the kinds of taps and patterns that would fit with the rhythm of the song.

Now, put on your tap shoes, play the song, and try some of the dance moves that you wrote down. Pay attention to which steps work and which ones don't.

Decide which moves you will use in your dance. What order will they go in?

In the box below, write out the first part of your dance. Use the "Step-Tap-Jump-Slide" notation you worked with on page 53.

My Tap Dance Choreography

Test your choreography by practicing it with a friend. Once you have your dance memorized, you will be ready to perform it!

Time

Write the time two ways. The first one is done for you.

1.

half past___**4**___

___**4:30**___

2.

half past_____

____:____

3.

half past_____

____:____

4.

half past_____

____:____

5.

half past_____

____:____

6.

half past_____

____:____

7.

half past_____

____:____

8.

half past_____

____:____

9.

half past_____

____:____

Use the context clues to make the best choice for each bold word's meaning.

1. Most small children are **forbidden** to cross the street without an adult.

    A. helped   B. told not to   C. forced

2. Tracy buttoned her **cardigan** to keep warm at the game.

    A. sweater   B. pajamas   C. boots

3. The autumn morning **dew** left the playground damp.

    A. clumps of dirt   B. pieces of ice   C. drops of water

4. Dad likes to **relax** on the sofa after he takes us swimming.

    A. jump   B. rest   C. eat

5. Our team must be **unified** if we want to win the championship.

    A. working together   B. awake   C. dressed up

6. I remember that type of butterfly by its **distinct** markings.

    A. yellow   B. special   C. dirty

7. The balloon **burst** as it brushed against the brick wall.

    A. flew higher   B. got away   C. popped

8. Some American Indians made the caves their **dwellings**.

    A. shoes   B. blankets   C. homes

FACTOID: Koalas sleep for up to 18 hours a day

Write the length of each object in centimeters.

1.

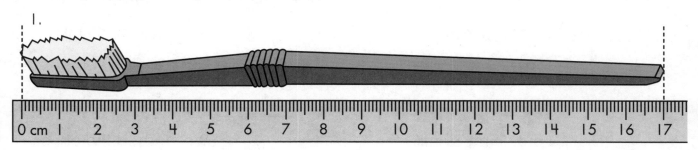

_____ centimeters

2.

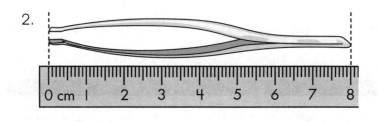

_____ centimeters

3.

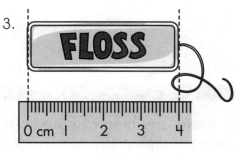

_____ centimeters

4.

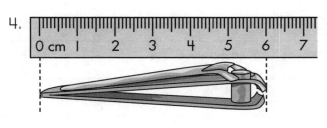

_____ centimeters

5.

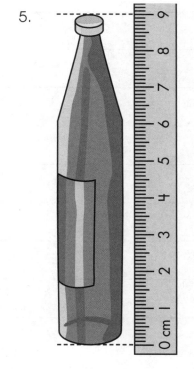

_____ centimeters

6.

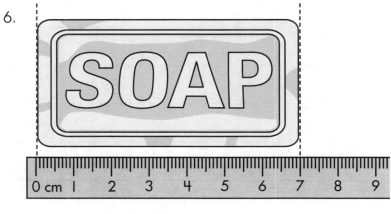

_____ centimeters

Read the sentence pairs. Write an X beside the sentence that happens first.

1. _____ I planted seeds.
   _____ The garden grew.

2. _____ Noah got on his bike.
   _____ Noah rode his bike.

3. _____ I put on my shoes.
   _____ I put on my pants.

4. _____ We ate our dinner.
   _____ We washed the dishes.

5. _____ I brushed my teeth.
   _____ I put toothpaste on my toothbrush.

6. _____ I climbed into bed.
   _____ I fell asleep.

Is there anything at your school that you think should be changed? Write a letter to your principal or teacher explaining your opinion. Include good reasons to support your opinion.

_____

_____

_____

_____

_____

_____

_____

_____

Subtract to solve each problem. Regroup if necessary.

1.   36
    − 17
	2. 98
	    − 19
		3. 28
		    − 9
			4. 41
			    − 15
				5. 33
				    − 17

1.   36 − 17

2.   98 − 19

3.   28 − 9

4.   41 − 15

5.   33 − 17

6.   72 − 53

7.   85 − 27

8.   43 − 29

9.   96 − 37

10. 64 − 36

11. 47 − 19

12. 94 − 26

13. 75 − 39

14. 61 − 22

15. 33 − 19

16. 71 − 46

17. 86 − 47

18. 94 − 35

19. 65 − 27

20. 92 − 44

21. 76 − 38

22. 64 − 35

23. 76 − 27

24. 52 − 44

25. 83 − 25

Bottle Bowling

Line up some empty plastic bottles on a wall. Stand a few feet away. Throw balls at the bottles and count how many times you throw before you hit all of them. Keep trying until the number of throws goes down.

Gather some balls near a sidewalk. Draw a chalk line and stand on it. Throw a ball as far away as you can. Ask a friend to put a stick on the spot where the ball landed. Do this several times, and then measure your longest throw.

Underline the root word in each word below. Then, write the definition of the word.

un = not	dis = not, opposite of
re = again	pre = before

1. disappear = _____

2. refill = _____

3. unlucky= _____

4. disloyal = _____

5. prepay = _____

6. unworthy = _____

7. rewrite = _____

8. prewash = _____

Reflexive pronouns **are special pronouns that end with** *–self* **or** *–selves*. **Circle the reflexive pronoun in each sentence.**

9. I told myself that we would stay dry, even if it rained.

10. The children were pleased with themselves for doing all their chores.

11. Grace made herself a tasty sandwich.

12. The kitten startled itself when it looked in the mirror.

13. After working all week, Ms. Chung gave herself the day off.

14. Did you give yourself a bath?

Read the time on the first clock. Write the same time on the second clock.

1.

```
 : 
 .
_____
```

2.

```
 : 
 .
_____
```

3.

```
 : 
 .
_____
```

4.

```
 : 
 .
_____
```

5.

```
 : 
 .
_____
```

6.

```
 : 
 .
_____
```

FITNESS FLASH: Make up a silly walk. What is the silliest way you can walk from your room to the front door?

Together, the letters *ph* make the /f/ sound. Read the sentences. Then, write the correct word from the word bank to complete each sentence.

| alphabet | amphibian | dolphins | phonics |

1. You are practicing _____ right now.

2. We saw _____ at the aquarium.

3. Becca wrote the letters of the _____.

4. A frog is an _____.

Add the prefix *un-* or *re-* to each word. Then, write the meaning of each new word.

5. pleasant _____

6. sure _____

7. able _____

8. write _____

9. build _____

10. print _____

Use addition or subtraction to solve each problem.

1. Anthony made 9 clay pots. He broke 4 of the pots. How many pots does he have left?

2. Keenan had 17 boxes of candy to sell. He sold 2 boxes to his grandma. His dad sold 9 boxes to people at work. How many more boxes did Keenan have to sell?

3. Min collects trading cards. She wants to collect all 15 cards in a series. She already has 8 of the cards. How many more cards does Min need?

4. Trina had 7 fish in her aquarium. She bought 4 more fish. How many fish does she have altogether?

5. Nina got 16 pieces of candy from the piñata. She ate 7 pieces. How many does she have left?

6. Bradley read 5 books the first month of summer break and 8 books the second month. How many books did he read in all?

FACTOID: The coldest temperature ever measured on Earth is −135.8 degrees Fahrenheit in Antarctica.

A Sunny Flower

Use details from the passage to complete the puzzle. If you are unsure of a word's meaning, use context clues to help you.

The sunflower grows from a seed. First, a sunflower plant begins to grow a strong taproot. Soon, the green stalk begins to grow toward the warmth of the sun. As the plant grows, it forms a bud that will someday become a flower. The plant faces the east as the sun rises in the morning. Then, it follows the sun across the sky until it is facing west when the sun sets. As the flower's bud blooms, it unfolds into large, golden petals. The center of the flower is full of seeds. The seeds are either eaten or planted so that more sunflowers can grow.

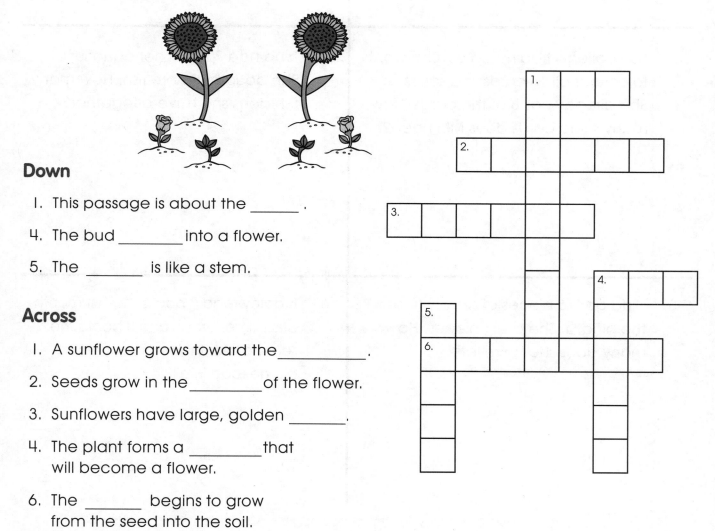

Down

1. This passage is about the _____.

4. The bud _____ into a flower.

5. The _____ is like a stem.

Across

1. A sunflower grows toward the_____.

2. Seeds grow in the _____ of the flower.

3. Sunflowers have large, golden _____.

4. The plant forms a _____ that will become a flower.

6. The _____ begins to grow from the seed into the soil.

Read each word. Then, circle the letter or letters that are silent.

1. wring

2. thumb

3. knee

4. knot

5. knife

6. bomb

7. dumb

8. knit

9. wrist

10. limb

11. gnaw

12. knead

Write each verb on the correct ladder.

EXAMPLE:

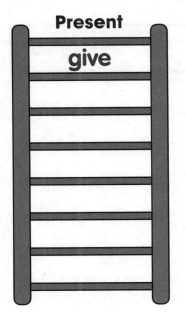

Present

give

broke   ride

break   laugh

find   laughed

found   wear

drew   wore

draw   ~~give~~

rode   ~~gave~~

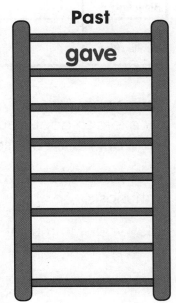

Past

gave

Exercise Enthusiasts, Final Step

Now, you are ready to create a weekly exercise calendar that you can use for the rest of the summer. This calendar will include all your favorite ways to exercise. Choose a set of activities that you will do every week. Make sure to include your goals for each exercise.

Amy's Weekly Exercise Calendar

	Sunday	Monday	Tuesday	Wednesday	Thursday	Friday	Saturday
Basketball			✔	✔	✔	✔	
Goal: 100 free throws a day	75	85	100	100	110	120	
Jump rope		✔	✔		✔	✔	
Goal: 15 minutes a day	10 min	15 min	20 min		15 min	15 min	5 min
Tag	✔					✔	
Goal: Twice a week for 30 minutes	45					30	
Bicycling		✔		✔			✔
Goal: Two 5-mile rides		6 miles		10 miles			5 miles

Notice how Amy only gave herself a checkmark for each exercise when she reached her exercise goal. Your goals should be challenging enough that you have to work at them but not so challenging that you will feel like giving up.

After you make your own exercise calendar, offer to make one for your fellow Exercise Enthusiasts, too.

Enjoy your summer of exercise!

Dance to the Rhythm, Final Step

You are almost ready to perform your dance!

First, you will need a stage for your performance. It could be your kitchen floor, the sidewalk, or a room at your local community center. Ask an adult for help choosing a spot.

You will also need sound equipment to play your song. It could be a CD player, a speaker dock for your smartphone, or something else. Ask an adult for help if you need it.

Finally, you will need to create a program to hand out to the members of your audience. Your program should include the date, time, and location of your performance. It should also include the title and singer of your song. Most importantly, it should include the name of the person who is performing the dance—that's you! You can also draw pictures for your program. Look at the next page for an example of how to make one. Then, use the box below to brainstorm ideas and sketch possible drawings.

Now, invite friends and family to watch you perform your dance! You could even record the performance and send a link to out-of-town friends and family as well. Happy tapping!

Dance Program Example

Here is an example of a program you could make for your tap dance performance:

Dance
to the
Rhythm

A Tap Dance Recital

by Monique Smith

Saturday, July 2

2 p.m.

Forestville Community Center

Program
"Happy" — Pharrell Williams

CHARACTER CHECK: Look for a chore at your house that needs to be done. Instead of waiting for someone else, volunteer to do it yourself.

Take It Outside!

If you have plastic eggs, drag them out for an ice hunt. Enclose an ice cube inside of each egg and hide the eggs in the yard. As your friends find the eggs, they should dump the ice into a wading pool. The last friend who dumps in some ice is the first one to jump into the wading pool! Brrr!

You never know what you will find under a rock. Take some paper and a pencil outside. Turn over a few rocks or small logs. Write down what scurries away. Put a tally mark next to any critter that you see more than once.

Can you predict the weather? If you look up and see low, thick clouds, then it may rain. If you see wispy, thin clouds high in the sky, the weather may be changing. If you see big, puffy clouds, it may storm later. So, what will your weather be like today?

State Snatcher

The State Snatcher has stolen some of the abbreviations of the states. Write the missing abbreviations. Use another U.S. map to help you.

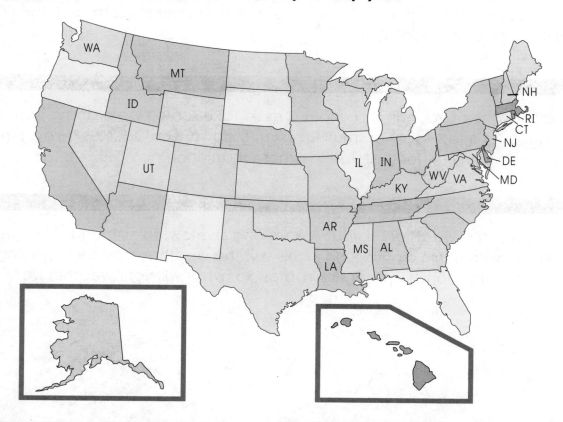

Postal Abbreviations Chart

Alabama	AL	Indiana	IN	Nebraska	NE	South Carolina	SC
Alaska	AK	Iowa	IA	Nevada	NV	South Dakota	SD
Arizona	AZ	Kansas	KS	New Hampshire	NH	Tennessee	TN
Arkansas	AR	Kentucky	KY	New Jersey	NJ	Texas	TX
California	CA	Louisiana	LA	New Mexico	NM	Utah	UT
Colorado	CO	Maine	ME	New York	NY	Vermont	VT
Connecticut	CT	Maryland	MD	North Carolina	NC	Virginia	VA
Delaware	DE	Massachusetts	MA	North Dakota	ND	Washington	WA
Florida	FL	Michigan	MI	Ohio	OH	West Virginia	WV
Georgia	GA	Minnesota	MN	Oklahoma	OK	Wisconsin	WI
Hawaii	HI	Mississippi	MS	Oregon	OR	Wyoming	WY
Idaho	ID	Missouri	MO	Pennsylvania	PA		
Illinois	IL	Montana	MT	Rhode Island	RI		

Section II Introduction

Theme: Travel and Learn

This month's explorations can be completed while traveling to places near and far. They encourage your child to build knowledge and make connections while visiting new and familiar places. Engage your child in family travel plans by looking at maps together, choosing destinations and activities, and reflecting on cultural experiences. Whether you travel to a family reunion, to a state or national park, or to another part of the world, you will find many opportunities to help your child learn during your adventures.

To build language arts and literacy skills this month, invite your child to help you use guidebooks, brochures, and websites to research travel destinations. Long car rides and waits at the airport are perfect opportunities to read books, tell stories, and play word games together. During your trip, purchase postcards and encourage your child to use them for writing simple messages to friends and relatives back home.

To build math skills this month, point out to your child the important role that numbers play in travel. Mile markers, gallons of gasoline purchased, hours traveled, time zone changes, and admission prices to attractions all make great real-world math lessons. Use situations from your travel adventures to invent simple addition and subtraction word problems for your child to solve. During road trips, notice numbers on license plates of passing vehicles and use them for more math practice.

Explorations

This month, your child will have a choice of two explorations. He may choose to follow steps for one or both. Review the explorations below with your child and help him make a choice. Emphasize that it is useful to have a path in mind from the start. Then, help your child find and complete the project activities according to his plan. Throughout the section, your child will see the icons shown below on pages that include directions directly related to one of the explorations. Emphasize that breaking a large project into smaller steps helps make it fun and easy to do.

 Take a Trip

With this exploration, your child will develop social studies, math, and writing skills as she plans an imaginary trip and creates a travel journal. She will exercise social studies skills as she researches destinations, consults atlases, and creates maps. She will call on math skills as she calculates distances and creates itineraries. And the research, organization, and descriptions needed to create a travel journal will help sharpen her writing and language arts skills.

You can help your child with this exploration by describing some of the places you have visited and enjoyed in the past. Ask your child to identify potential destinations in an atlas or guidebook and describe what she would like to do there. And as you visit real-life places this summer, have your child practice describing those places in writing.

Someone Else's Shoes

With this exploration, your child will develop his powers of observation, vocabulary, science, and writing skills as he thinks about what it might be like to "walk in someone else's shoes." He will be choosing an animal or insect to research and observe. After gathering information and observations, he will use his imagination to create a character based on the animal. Then, he will call on his language arts skills to write and perform a movie scene starring that character.

You can help your child with this exploration by joining him as he observes his animal in the backyard, at the zoo, or at a park. Come up with different scenarios and challenge your child to think about what the animal might do in each one. Ask your child to think about which actor or actress he would want to be the voice of the animal character for the movie scene he is writing.

Learning Activities

Practice pages for this month move from second grade review to an introduction of third grade skills. They also focus on skills that support the explorations described above. Preview the activities and choose several that target skills your child needs to practice. Also select several relating to the exploration(s) your child plans to complete. You may wish to mark those pages with a star or other symbol to let your child know to begin with those. Then, let your child choose practice activities that interest her and allow her to demonstrate her growing skills.

Take a Trip, Step I

Even if you are staying home this summer, you can travel anywhere using your imagination! In this exploration, you will plan a trip you would like to make. It can be a journey to one place or an extended trip with lots of stops. At the end of the month, you will use drawings or photos to create a journal of your extended trip!

Use this box to brainstorm where to go on your trip. List all the places you would like to visit. Use an atlas or the Internet to find each place on a map. Make a checkmark next to each place after you locate it. Do you want to try to visit every one of them on this trip, or would you rather focus on just a few places? When you have decided, write "Yes" next to the places you will include on your trip.

1. _____

2. _____

3. _____

4. _____

5. _____

6. _____

7. _____

8. _____

9. _____

10. _____

Someone Else's Shoes, Step 1

Have you ever wondered what it would be like to experience life as an animal or an insect? In this exploration, you can find out! You will observe and research the life of an animal or insect you are curious about. Then, you will use your imagination to create an animal or insect "character." Finally, you will write a movie scene about your life as this character and perform it for your friends and family.

First, think about which animal or insect you would like to explore. Use the lines below to list the ones you are most interested in.

_____

Once you have chosen an animal or insect, use the lines below to write about what interests you most about it:

_____

Draw a picture of your animal or insect in the space below.

Color My World

Is it a city, state, country, continent or body of water? Color each box according to the Color Key. Use an atlas for help.

Color Key

city—orange	state—green	country—yellow
water—blue	continent—purple	

Atlantic Ocean	India	Colorado	Miami
Peru	Antarctica	Lake Michigan	Hawaii
New Orleans	Spain	Europe	Gulf of Mexico
Vermont	Phoenix	Japan	Paris
East China Sea	Egypt	Wyoming	Sweden
Africa	London	Hudson Bay	Connecticut
Greece	Minnesota	South America	Dallas
Oakland	Great Salt Lake	Argentina	Arctic Ocean
North America	Canada	Chicago	Arkansas
Lake Victoria	Iowa	Asia	Venezuela
Lima	Persian Gulf	Mexico	Moscow
Pacific Ocean	Maryland	Cincinnati	Brazil

Add to solve each problem.

1. Mischa has 9 ![]. Uma has 12 ![]. Quinton has 26 ![].

   How many ![] do they have in all? _____

2. The toy store sold 12 ![] in April,

   15 ![] in May, and 20 ![] in June.

   How many ![] did the toy store sell in all? _____

3. Geneva puts 6 ![], 19 ![], and

   29 ![] on shelves. How many toys

   does Geneva put on shelves? _____

4. The toy store has 31 ![], 16 ![],

   and 26 ![]. How many of these toys

   does the toy store have in all? _____

5. The bakery sells 12 ![] on Thursday, 22 ![]

   on Friday, and 31 ![] on Saturday.

   How many ![] did the bakery sell? _____

Draw a line to match each present-tense verb with its past-tense form.

1. freeze   held

2. hold   fell

3. catch   spoke

4. run   bought

5. speak   froze

6. fall   caught

7. buy   ran

Rewrite each set of underlined words using a possessive noun. The first one is done for you.

8. The book belonging to Connor is on the shelf.   **Connor's book**

9. Have you seen the basketball belonging to Ivan? _____

10. I forgot to bring the snorkel belonging to Tiffany. _____

11. The pie plates belonging to Grandma are in the basement. _____

12. The ballet shoes belonging to Chandra are too small. _____

13. Halley left the tennis racquet belonging to Morgan on the bus. _____

Practice "counting on" using the coins shown.

1.

____¢ ____¢ ____¢ ____¢ ____¢ ____¢ ____¢ ____¢   Total ____¢

2.

____¢ ____¢ ____¢ ____¢ ____¢ ____¢ ____¢ ____¢   Total ____¢

3.

____¢ ____¢ ____¢ ____¢ ____¢ ____¢ ____¢ ____¢   Total ____¢

4.

____¢ ____¢ ____¢ ____¢ ____¢ ____¢ ____¢ ____¢   Total ____¢

5.

____¢ ____¢ ____¢ ____¢ ____¢ ____¢ ____¢ ____¢   Total ____¢

6.

____¢ ____¢ ____¢ ____¢ ____¢ ____¢ ____¢ ____¢   Total ____¢

FITNESS FLASH: Find a soft surface and do five somersaults.

Read the passage. Then, answer the questions.

Some people save stamps. They keep their stamps in albums. They like to look at them. Some people like stamps that are very old. Some people like pretty stamps. Some people like stamps from places that are far away. Some stamps are worth a lot of money. Stamps that were printed incorrectly can be worth the most.

1. Where do some people keep their stamps?

   _____

2. What is one reason people keep stamps?

   _____

3. Name two kinds of stamps that people keep.

   _____

4. What kinds of stamps can be worth the most?

   _____

CHARACTER CHECK: What would you do if you heard your classmates teasing or making fun of someone?

Create a line plot using the length of each shape.

4 in.

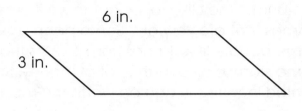

6 in.

3 in.

9 in.

3 in.

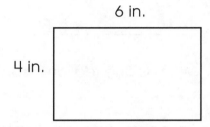

6 in.

4 in.

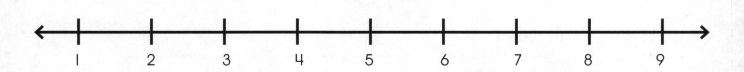

Read the sentences. Look at each underlined word. Then, color in the circle to tell if the word is spelled correctly or incorrectly.

EXAMPLE:

		CORRECT	INCORRECT
	We <u>ate</u> biscuits with butter on them.	●	○
1.	We <u>wint</u> to the store for some cereal and milk.	○	○
2.	The cat will chase a <u>mouse</u>.	○	○
3.	We will <u>plant</u> our flower bed.	○	○
4.	The <u>keng</u> asked the queen to dance.	○	○
5.	<u>Think</u> of a good name for a puppy.	○	○

Imagine that you are collecting items for a time capsule that will be opened in 20 years. What things would you put in the capsule to tell about your life right now?

_____

_____

_____

_____

_____

_____

_____

_____

_____

Estimate how many inches long each object is.

inches | 1   2   3   4   5   6   7

1. _____ inch

2.  _____ inches

3.  _____ inches

4.  _____ inches

5. _____ inches

6.

_____ inches

Read each pair of sentences. If they tell how Sara's life is the same as Katie's, circle the word *same*. If they tell how Sara's life is different from Katie's, circle the word *different*.

A girl named Katie lives in a desert town not far from Sara's home. In some ways, Katie's life is like Sara's. In other ways, their lives are very different.

1.	Sara is a tortoise. Katie is a human.	same	different
2.	Sara lives in a burrow. Katie lives in a house.	same	different
3.	Sara eats in the morning. Katie does, too.	same	different
4.	Sara can live for more than 60 years. Katie can, too.	same	different
5.	Sara does not have wings. Katie doesn't either.	same	different
6.	Sara can go for years without drinking water. Katie needs water every day.	same	different
7.	Sara sleeps all winter. Katie does not.	same	different
8.	Sara has four legs. Katie has two.	same	different

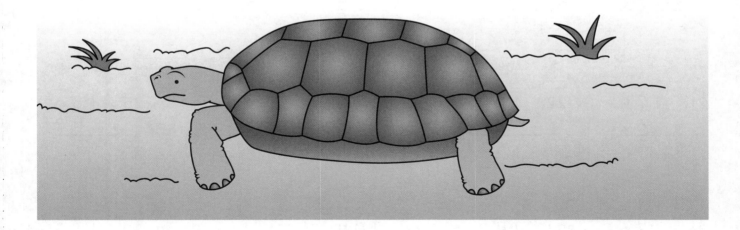

FITNESS FLASH: Stand up, place your hands on your hips, and rotate your upper body as far as you can in each direction. Make sure not to jerk your body or move too fast!

Subtract to solve the problems.

1. 123   2. 196   3. 165   4. 163   5. 119
   − 61   − 87   − 59   − 71   − 29

6. 106   7. 100   8. 153   9. 174   10. 192
   − 51   − 29   − 69   − 87   − 75

11. 157   12. 169   13. 142   14. 140   15. 113
   − 59   − 99   − 37   − 93   − 37

16. 167   17. 173   18. 129   19. 143   20. 126
   − 76   − 82   − 94   − 77   − 54

21. 174   22. 100   23. 175   24. 142   25. 136
   − 62   − 33   − 46   − 57   − 47

26. 176   27. 143   28. 104   29. 173   30. 163
   − 89   − 54   − 29   − 75   − 92

Write the past-tense form of each verb to complete each sentence.

1. Caleb _____ a card for Mason.
   (buy)

2. Jayla _____ her dog to the park.
   (take)

3. She _____ enough bread for a week.
   (make)

4. Daysha and I _____ the movie last night.
   (see)

5. I _____ to the grocery store.
   (go)

6. The bird _____ to the nest.
   (fly)

Write *am*, *is*, or *are* to complete each sentence.

7. I _____ the tallest girl in my class.

8. My lunch _____ in my backpack.

9. We _____ in line for the roller coaster.

10. I _____ ready to go biking.

11. Jacob's friends _____ laughing at a joke.

12. Aunt Davetta _____ listening to the radio.

13. We _____ painting the room green.

FACTOID: The human body contains about 60,000 miles of blood vessels.

85

Take a Trip, Step 2

It's time to map out a route for your trip!

What you'll need:
- the list of places you will be visiting
- sheets of paper
- tape
- markers, colored pencils, or crayons
- ruler

What to do:
1. Grab a piece of paper to draw your map on. Or, you can use the space provided on the next page.

2. Draw a map that includes your home and all of the places you've decided to visit. If you want to make a bigger map, you can use tape to fasten together two or more pieces of paper.

3. Number the places in the order you want to visit them. The last number should be your home.

4. Next to each place you have marked on the map, draw a picture of something you will see when you visit.

5. Show your route. Use a ruler to draw a line from your home to "1" on the map, from "1" to "2," and so on.

6. Use an atlas to figure out the distances between your destinations. Use addition to find out how many total miles you will be traveling.

Tell how you will you travel to the places you are visiting. Can you take a car, or will you ride in a train, a boat, or an airplane?

_____

_____

_____

_____

_____

Take a Trip, Step 2

BONUS

Blood on the Move

The circulatory system is responsible for moving blood through the body. This system also carries disease-fighting substances that help prevent you from getting sick.

The main components of your body's circulatory system are the heart, blood vessels, blood, and the lymphatic system. Your heart controls this system.

The heart's constant pumping is responsible for sending oxygen-rich blood to the rest of your body through blood vessels called arteries. Blood vessels called veins return blood to your heart. Your veins look blue because the blood in them has no oxygen. Back toward the heart, the blood gathers more oxygen as it passes through your lungs and becomes red. This cycle occurs about once every minute.

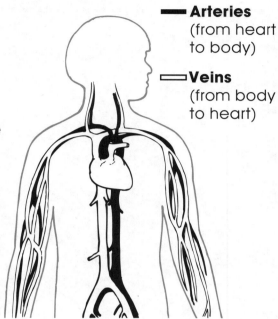

Arteries
(from heart to body)

Veins
(from body to heart)

Directions:
Use the information above to solve the puzzle.

Across:

2. The _____ controls the circulatory system.
4. Blood without oxygen is _____.
6. Arteries carry blood mixed with _____ from the heart to the rest of the body.
7. _____ carry blood to the heart.

Down:

1. _____ carry blood away from the heart.
3. Blood is _____ when it contains oxygen.
5. Blood gets oxygen from your _____.

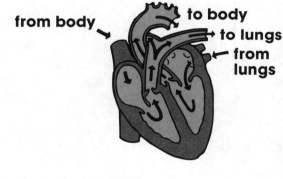

from body   to body
to lungs
from lungs

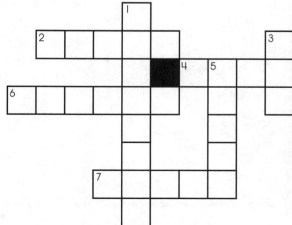

Symbols of America's Heritage

Written in the box below are names of some symbols of America's heritage. Below the box are pictures of these symbols. Write the name for each symbol on the line under its picture. Color each picture as you are directed.

Liberty Bell	Washington Monument	Statue of Liberty
The White House	United States Capitol	Mount Rushmore
U.S. Flag	Gateway Arch	Bald Eagle

1.

_____
Color me silver.

2.

_____
Color me red, white, and blue.

3.

_____
Color me brown.

4.

_____
Color me white.

5.

_____
Color me tan.

6.

_____
Color me brown, white and yellow.

7.

_____
Color me green.

8.

_____
Color me gray.

9.

_____
Color me white.

BONUS

Take It Outside!

Go on a texture hunt. Peel the paper off of a dark crayon. Grab a piece of paper and head outside. Put the paper on tree trunks, sidewalks, and patio furniture. Rub the crayon over the paper. Ask a friend to guess where each rubbing came from.

Insects and other animals transfer yellow dust called pollen from flower to flower. This helps plants grow fruit. Sit outside and watch some flowers. List all of the animals that land on them.

Grab some sidewalk chalk and go outside with a friend on a bright day. Stand on a sunny sidewalk next to each other, and write an X to mark where each of you is standing. Then, have your friend make a silly pose. Trace your friend's shadow with chalk. Then, make a silly pose yourself and ask your friend to trace your shadow. Try to make the same poses and "fit" back into the tracings.

Wait two hours and then return to your Xs on the sidewalk. Make your poses again, and notice how your shadows have changed. Do they still fit inside the chalk tracings? Have they gotten taller or shorter?

Study the shapes. Then, answer each question.

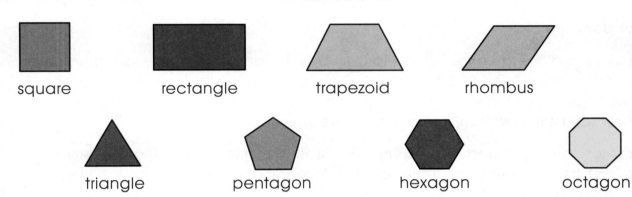

square   rectangle   trapezoid   rhombus   circle

triangle   pentagon   hexagon   octagon

1. Which shapes are quadrilaterals (shapes with four sides)?

   _____   _____

   _____   _____

2. Name a quadrilateral with four equal sides. _____

3. What shape has three sides and three angles? _____

4. What shape has no sides? _____

5. What shape has five sides? _____

6. What shape has six sides? _____

7. What shape has eight sides? _____

8. What shapes have two or more parallel sides?

   _____   _____

   _____   _____

   _____   _____

9. How is a trapezoid different from a rhombus? _____

   _____

   _____

The Ostrich

Read the passage.

The ostrich is a unique bird. It is the largest bird. It can grow to be eight feet tall and can weigh more than 200 pounds. Unlike most other birds, the ostrich cannot fly. Its long legs help it run very fast. It runs with its wings outstretched. It uses its strong legs to protect itself, and it will run or kick if threatened.

The ostrich lays eggs and has feathers like other birds. Its eggs are extremely large. In fact, its eggs are almost the size of a football and can weigh nearly three pounds. The male ostrich digs a hole in the ground for a nest. The female ostrich lays her eggs in the hole. Then, both parents protect the eggs until the chicks hatch. Often, the female sits on the eggs during the day, and the male sits on the eggs during the night. After the chicks hatch, the parents continue to be very protective until the chicks can take care of themselves.

Use the passage to answer the questions.

1. Circle the letter of the sentence that tells the main idea.
    A. The ostrich is the largest bird.
    B. The ostrich is one of the most unique of all birds.
    C. The ostrich lays eggs and has feathers like other birds.

2. Write a *T* if the sentence is true. Write an *F* if the sentence is false.
    _____ A. The ostrich can fly.
    _____ B. The ostrich can run very fast.
    _____ C. The mother ostrich lays its eggs in a hole in the ground.
    _____ D. The ostrich cannot kick without falling down.

3. Compare the ostrich to other birds. Put an *X* in the boxes to show whether each characteristic describes the ostrich, other birds, or both.

ostrich		other birds
☐	can fly	☐
☐	has/have feathers	☐
☐	lays eggs	☐
☐	grows to be 8 feet tall	☐
☐	protective of young	☐

4. Complete each sentence by circling the correct homophone.

    The ostrich can grow to be _____ feet tall.
           ate   eight

    The ostrich can weigh more than _____ hundred pounds.
           too   two

    The ostrich egg can _____ nearly three pounds.
           way   weigh

    The _____ ostrich digs a hole in the ground for the nest.
           mail   male

The ending *-er* sometimes means "more." It may be used to compare two things. The ending *-est* means "most." It is used to compare more than two things. If a word ends in *e*, only add *-r* or *-st* to the word. Write the appropriate ending in each blank.

5. The ostrich is large____ than most birds.
6. It is probably the tall____ of all birds.
7. Ostrich eggs are the large____ eggs in the world.
8. Its powerful legs make it the fast____ bird on the ground.

What fraction of each figure is shaded?

1.

   _____

2.

   _____

3.

   _____

4.

   _____

5.

   _____

6.

   _____

7.

   _____

8.

   _____

9.

   _____

10.

    _____

11.

    _____

12.

    _____

FITNESS FLASH: Lie on your stomach with your legs straight. Put your forearms and palms flat on the floor. Lift your body up and balance on your forearms and toes. Do this for 10 seconds.

Solve each problem.

1. The small hand is between _____ and _____ .

   The large hand is on the _____ .

   The time is _____ **:** _____ .

2. The small hand is between _____ and _____ .

   The large hand is on the _____ .

   The time is _____ **:** _____ .

3. The small hand is on the _____ .

   The large hand is on the _____ .

   The time is _____ **:** _____ .

4. The small hand is on the _____ .

   The large hand is on the _____ .

   The time is _____ **:** _____ .

5. The small hand is between _____ and _____ .

   The large hand is on the _____ .

   The time is _____ **:** _____ .

Look at each underlined word. On the line, write whether it is a *noun*, *pronoun*, *verb*, *adjective*, or *adverb*.

1. _____ The old blue <u>tent</u> smelled of leaves and woodsy air.

2. _____ Dad <u>carefully</u> unzipped the tent's windows.

3. _____ The smell of <u>crispy</u> bacon filled the air.

4. _____ A clear stream <u>ran</u> along one side of the campsite.

5. _____ <u>I</u> couldn't wait to start the campfire.

6. _____ We <u>roasted</u> hot dogs and marshmallows.

Add the missing commas to each address below. Use this symbol to add them: ⌃.

7. 81 Riverbrook Rd.
    Grand Rapids MI 49505

8. 132 West Billingsley Lane
    Taos NM 87571

9. 1425 Newman Terrace
    Des Moines IA 50328

10. 21896 Landon Blvd.
    Orlando FL 32807

11. 10346 State Route 39
    Tuscaloosa AL 35401

12. 992 Rabbit Run Rd.
    Champaign IL 61826

CHARACTER CHECK: Have you made any promises to friends or family members lately? What are some ways you can take responsibility and keep your word to them?

Add to solve each problem.

1. 182
    + 703

2. 231
    + 547

3. 825
    + 163

4. 436
    + 562

5. 325
    + 202

6. 274
    + 320

7. 641
    + 345

8. 908
    + 61

9. 365
    + 424

10. 207
    + 712

11. 352
    + 436

12. 475
    + 510

13. 724
    + 143

14. 650
    + 227

15. 298
    + 500

16. 525
    + 261

17. 631
    + 155

18. 447
    + 432

19. 319
    + 450

20. 752
    + 136

21. 933
    + 52

22. 547
    + 131

23. 830
    + 69

24. 626
    + 331

25. 487
    + 411

26. 631
    + 325

27. 488
    + 211

28. 562
    + 407

29. 723
    + 166

30. 506
    + 353

FITNESS FLASH: Jump up and down in one spot for 30 seconds. How high can you go?

The Story of Soap

Soap has been around for a long time. Babylonians were the first known culture to use soap. They lived more than 4,000 years ago. Babylonians made soap by mixing water, alkali, and cassia oil together.

In the late 19th century, manufactured soap bars became available in Europe and the United States. The advertising campaigns used by the manufacturers to sell their soaps helped increase public awareness of the importance of good hygiene and its relationship to good health.

By the 1950s, soap had become an important instrument for personal hygiene. Today, soap is used for cleaning clothes, dishes, cars, floors, and so much more.

1. What was the first known culture to use soap?

    _____

2. Where were manufactured soap bars first available?

    _____

3. Why is good hygiene important?

    _____

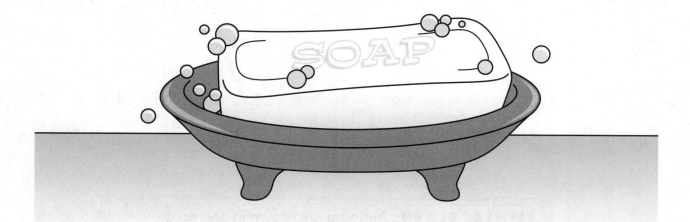

Create a line plot based on the measurements below.

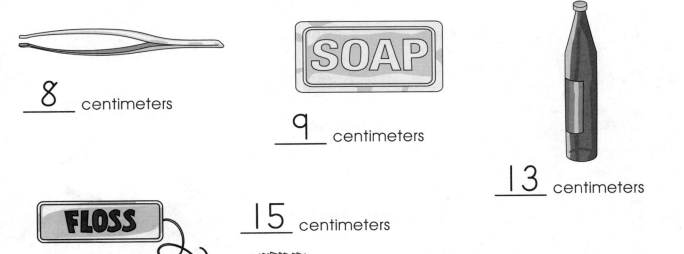

___8___ centimeters

___9___ centimeters

___13___ centimeters

___6___ centimeters

___15___ centimeters

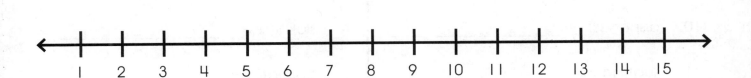

1 2 3 4 5 6 7 8 9 10 11 12 13 14 15

Write *has* or *have* to complete each sentence.

1. We _____ fun ideas for this vacation.

2. My dad _____ Monday off.

3. My mom _____ a new book.

4. The girl _____ a hat.

5. Lin and I _____ pears in our lunches.

6. The doghouses _____ new roofs.

7. His sister _____ tap shoes.

8. The club _____ many members.

Use the prefix and suffix meanings in the box to help you write a definition for each word.

un/non = not	er/or = one who
re = again	tion = act or process of
dis = not, opposite of	ness = state or condition of

9. fighter = _____

10. dishonest = _____

11. subtraction = _____

12. nonfiction = _____

13. unwise = _____

14. sickness = _____

15. collector = _____

16. reuse = _____

Find the perimeter of each shape.

1.
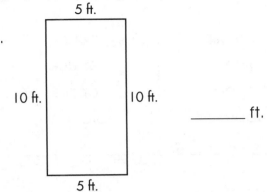
5 ft.

10 ft.   10 ft.

5 ft.

_____ ft.

2.
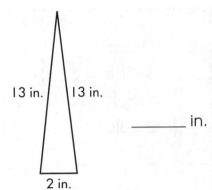
13 in.   13 in.

2 in.

_____ in.

3.
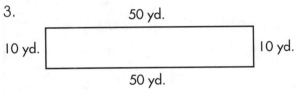
50 yd.

10 yd.   10 yd.

50 yd.

_____ yd.

4.
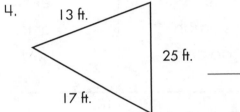
13 ft.

25 ft.

17 ft.

_____ ft.

Find the unknown side.

5.
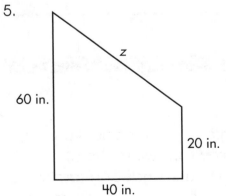
z

60 in.

20 in.

40 in.

P = __150__ in.

z = _____ in.

6.
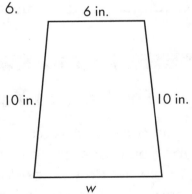
6 in.

10 in.   10 in.

w

P = __34__ in.

w = _____ in.

7.
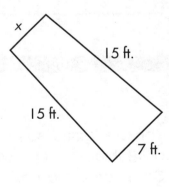
x

15 ft.

15 ft.

7 ft.

P = __42__ in.

x = _____ in.

Cross out the word that does not belong in each group.

1.	2.	3.	4.
boot sandal sock sneaker	Uranus Orion Big Dipper Little Dipper	paper clip glue orange tape	celery lettuce apple broccoli
5.	6.	7.	8.
catfish tuna salmon dolphin	pink yellow blue red	candle mirror flashlight lantern	heart green leprechaun clover
9.	10.	11.	12.
ears eyes nose arm	stairs pit step stool ladder	shirt socks pants window	book magazine baseball menu

The Best of You

You are terrific, so put it down on paper! Make a list of 10 great things about yourself, or 10 things you do well. Maybe you make an amazing turkey sandwich, win at Checkers almost every time, or always do your best to help your friends and family. Tape the list up in your room and read it often, especially when you're feeling down. Remember all the great things that make you, you!

Add to solve each problem. Regroup if necessary.

1. 283 + 168	2. 497 + 205	3. 176 + 640	4. 325 + 867	5. 651 + 179
6. 304 + 519	7. 517 + 334	8. 237 + 807	9. 482 + 531	10. 117 + 488
11. 624 + 276	12. 431 + 382	13. 329 + 682	14. 772 + 405	15. 532 + 489
16. 136 + 477	17. 479 + 342	18. 379 + 483	19. 386 + 364	20. 670 + 259
21. 823 + 357	22. 937 + 468	23. 736 + 136	24. 648 + 246	25. 462 + 369
26. 837 + 337	27. 689 + 285	28. 350 + 261	29. 427 + 367	30. 601 + 289

Circle the root word in each word below. Then, think of another word that has the same root. Write the new word on the line.

1. reasonable _____

2. uninteresting _____

3. misbehavior _____

4. unbelievable _____

5. bicyclist _____

6. telephone _____

Which character from a book that you have read is most like you? How are you and this character alike?

_____

_____

_____

_____

_____

_____

Write each time two ways.

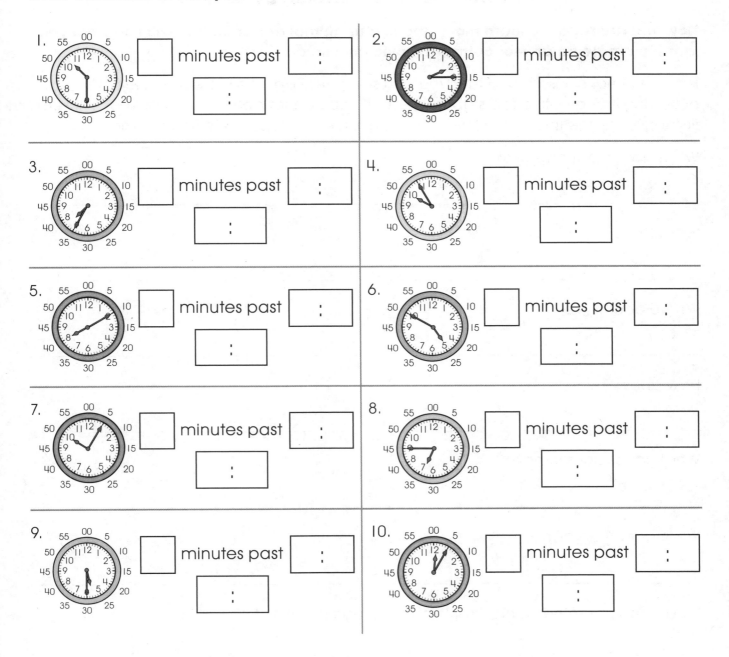

1. ☐ minutes past ☐:

☐:

2. ☐ minutes past ☐:

☐:

3. ☐ minutes past ☐:

☐:

4. ☐ minutes past ☐:

☐:

5. ☐ minutes past ☐:

☐:

6. ☐ minutes past ☐:

☐:

7. ☐ minutes past ☐:

☐:

8. ☐ minutes past ☐:

☐:

9. ☐ minutes past ☐:

☐:

10. ☐ minutes past ☐:

☐:

FITNESS FLASH: Kneel with your toes touching and your knees spread apart. Slowly bend down, touch your forehead to the floor, and hold it there for 10 seconds.

Someone Else's Shoes, Step 2

Now you are ready to learn more about your animal or insect. You will use what you learn to create an animal or insect movie character!

Is your animal or insect one that you can see in real life? If so, spend some time observing it and noting facts about its life. If you cannot observe your animal or insect firsthand, use the Internet, a library book, or an encyclopedia to find out more.

What does it eat and drink?

_____

What does it look like?

_____

Where does it live?

_____

How does it move?

_____

What noises does it make?

_____

What does it do all day?

_____

What are some other interesting things you learned about it?

_____

Someone Else's Shoes, Step 2

Now it is time to create your movie character!

Answering these questions will help you decide what your animal or insect character will be like.

What is your character's name?

_____

Who are its friends and family? Who are its enemies?

_____

What does it want to do the most?

_____

What is it afraid of?

_____

What motivates your character?

_____

What are some of your character's good qualities? What are some of its bad qualities?

_____

How would you feel if you were the character?

_____

Did you think of any other details about your character? Write them in the brainstorming box:

```




```

I Can Feel My Heartbeat

Each time your heart pumps the blood through veins and arteries, you can feel it! It's called a pulse. You can feel your pulse in two places where the arteries are close to the surface of your skin. Gently, place two fingers on the inside of your wrist or on your neck next to your windpipe. Silently count the pulses and complete the chart below.

* An adult should time and direct each part. Time for 6 seconds and then multiply by 10.

Pulse Rate	Sitting	Walking around room for 1 minute	Wait 2 minutes, then standing	After 25 jumping jacks	Wait 1 minute, then lying down	After jogging in place for 2 minutes	After resting for 5 minutes
In 6 seconds							
In 1 minute							

You should have found that your heart beats faster when you are active. That's because your body uses more oxygen when it exercises, and the blood must circulate faster to get more oxygen to your muscles! With your family or friends, compare pulse rates and find the average (using the 1-minute rate).

Pulse Rate	Sitting	After walking	After standing	After jumping	After lying down	After jogging	After resting
You							
Person #2							
Person #3							
Total							
÷ 3 to find average							

Up the Lazy River

"The steamboat is coming!" was a cry heard in the many small river towns in the 1800s. Steamboats carried people and packages along the waterways before the faster railroads were developed.

The shipping tags below tell where each package is beginning and ending its journey. Use a map, atlas, or other reference book to find the river on which the steamboat will be traveling. Some steamboats may have to travel on more than one river.

Directions: Write the name of the river routes on each shipping tag.

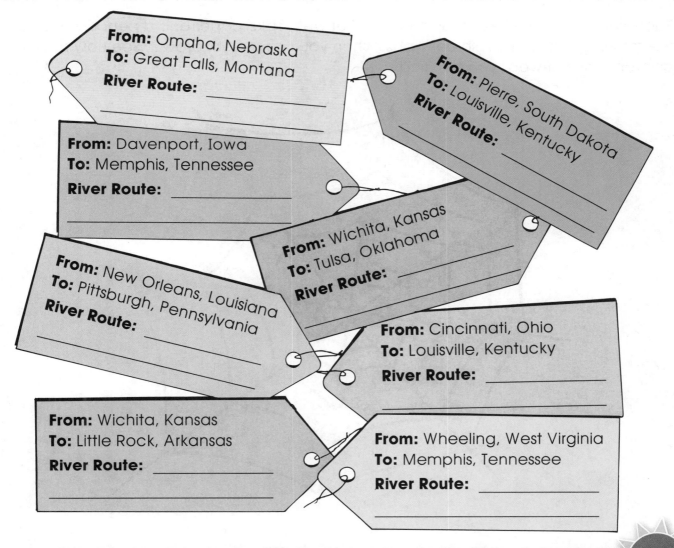

From: Omaha, Nebraska
To: Great Falls, Montana
River Route: _____
_____

From: Pierre, South Dakota
To: Louisville, Kentucky
River Route: _____

From: Davenport, Iowa
To: Memphis, Tennessee
River Route: _____
_____

From: Wichita, Kansas
To: Tulsa, Oklahoma
River Route: _____

From: New Orleans, Louisiana
To: Pittsburgh, Pennsylvania
River Route: _____
_____

From: Cincinnati, Ohio
To: Louisville, Kentucky
River Route: _____

From: Wichita, Kansas
To: Little Rock, Arkansas
River Route: _____
_____

From: Wheeling, West Virginia
To: Memphis, Tennessee
River Route: _____
_____

BONUS

Take It Outside!

Help birds build nests. Gather yarn, fabric strips, twigs, and newspaper strips. Tie them in a loose bundle. Tie the bundle to a tree branch. Do you see nests in your area that include the goodies you provided?

You do not need a partner to play tennis. Pick up a racket and ball and find a wall. The wall should be at least 10 feet high with no windows. Toss the ball in the air and hit it against the wall. See how many times you can hit the ball without missing.

Each kind of spider makes a different kind of web. Take paper and a pencil outside in the morning and look for spider webs. When you find a web, draw it. See how many different kinds of webs you can find.

The Midnight Ride

Number the sentences 1–6 to retell the story below in sequence.

It was early morning on April 19, 1775. Paul Revere and many other colonists were ready to fight against the British army. They called themselves *minutemen* because they would need to be ready to fight at a minute's notice. First, Paul waited for a signal from the American spies. They knew the British army would eventually move toward Lexington and Concord, but they did not know whether the British would travel by land or across the water. When the spies told Paul, he would send a signal to the other minutemen, telling them from which direction the British were attacking. Next, he would ride his horse quickly through the farmland and towns, shouting the news that the British were coming.

At last, the word came from the spies. Paul immediately ordered two lanterns to be hung in the tall tower of the church, a signal that meant the British were attacking by sea. Then, he mounted his horse and rode fast into the night. Paul Revere knew the importance of warning the minutemen to prepare for battle. The British army had more men and more guns, so the minutemen would need to surprise them. Paul rode through Lexington, shouting the news. But, as he rode out of town, he was caught by the British. Meanwhile, two other riders made it further and told the minutemen to be ready to fight in Concord.

Soon, the British army reached Concord. They had no idea that the minutemen were waiting. They were surprised and fled the area. The minutemen that were awakened had won their first fight.

_____ Paul Revere was caught by a British soldier.

_____ Two lanterns were lit in the church tower.

_____ Paul Revere rode through Lexington.

_____ The minutemen surprised the British army in Concord.

_____ Paul Revere received word from the spies.

_____ Two other American riders warned the minutemen to gather in Concord.

Subtract to solve each problem.

1. 684
   − 253

2. 634
   − 421

3. 835
   − 610

4. 738
   − 502

5. 325
   − 102

6. 874
   − 321

7. 647
   − 325

8. 958
   − 146

9. 363
   − 242

10. 567
   − 362

11. 283
   − 220

12. 488
   − 351

13. 695
   − 233

14. 719
   − 305

15. 894
   − 752

16. 975
   − 342

17. 767
   − 425

18. 836
   − 132

19. 547
   − 235

20. 658
   − 510

21. 393
   − 173

22. 649
   − 235

23. 786
   − 526

24. 999
   − 683

25. 887
   − 346

Jump and Sing

Grab a jump rope if you have one, or borrow one from a friend. As you are jumping, sing one of your favorite songs. Try to keep jumping rope without stumbling until you finish the song. As you get better, try singing longer songs. Have a friend time you to see how long you can jump. If you have friends who like to jump rope, too, you could even put on a jump-rope concert!

Add the suffixes -ed and -ing to each base word. You may need to drop letters from or add letters to some words before adding the suffixes.

1. fake	2. jump	3. kiss	4. cook	5. grate
_____	_____	_____	_____	_____
_____	_____	_____	_____	_____

6. wrap	7. snooze	8. pop	9. talk	10. grin
_____	_____	_____	_____	_____
_____	_____	_____	_____	_____

Write the letter of the correct definition next to each word.

1. _____ cheerful

2. _____ hopeless

3. _____ doubtful

4. _____ sunless

5. _____ helpful

A. ready to help

B. without sun

C. very cheery

D. having doubts

E. without hope

Estimate how many centimeters long each object is.

1.

 _____ cm

2.

 _____ cm

3.

 _____ cm

4.

 _____ cm

5.

 _____ cm

6.

 _____ cm

Solve each problem. The first one is done for you.

1. Maurice had 3 dimes.

   He found 5 pennies in the couch cushions.

   How much money does Maurice have now? __**35¢**__

2. Trisha has 3 nickels.

   Brandi has 11 pennies.

   How much money do they have altogether? _____

3. Addie has 1 dime and 7 pennies.

   How much money does she have? _____

4. Ashton pulls 2 one-dollar bills, 1 quarter, 1 dime, 3 nickels, and 9 pennies from his piggy bank.

   How much money does Ashton have? _____

5. Bailey's mother put a one-dollar bill, 2 quarters, 3 dimes, 1 nickel, and 7 pennies in an envelope for Bailey to use at the county fair.

   How much money did Bailey's
   mother give her for the county fair? _____

Bicycle Safety

Read the passage.

Many people have been hurt while enjoying bicycle rides. Bicycle accidents can be very serious. It is important to learn the safety rules of owning and riding a bicycle. These safety rules are so important that some schools and communities offer bicycle safety courses.

It is important that your bicycle is in good condition before you ride. The tires should have good tread and the correct air pressure. The brakes, the handlebars, and the pedals should all function correctly. If any of these parts do not operate correctly, do not ride the bicycle. You should fix the bicycle first.

After checking your bicycle, make sure that you have the right safety equipment. Reflectors, a bicycle helmet, bright clothing, and laced shoes are important safety requirements to ride a bicycle.

Reflectors and bright clothing help drivers and other riders to see you. A bicycle helmet will protect your head if you fall off of the bicycle. To prevent your shoelaces from getting stuck in the bicycle's spokes or the chain, be sure that your shoes are properly laced and tied securely.

After you have an operating bicycle and safety equipment, you are ready to ride. When you are riding, be sure to ride with the direction of traffic. Never ride against traffic. Follow all traffic signs. Use arm signals to give advance warning to others of the direction you are turning.

Car drivers, other bicyclists, and pedestrians don't always pay attention to bicycle riders. That is why it is so important for bicycle riders to pay attention to everything around them and to follow bicycle safety tips. A safe rider is a happy rider. Have fun!

Use the passage to answer the questions.

1. Why is it important to obey bicycle safety rules?

    _____

2. When should you wear bright clothing?

    A. during the day   C. every time you ride

    B. during the evening   D. never

3. What parts on the bicycle should you check before riding?

    _____

4. What safety equipment should you use when you ride?

    _____

    _____

5. On which side of the street should you ride your bike?

    A. with the direction of traffic

    B. the left side

    C. on the sidewalk

    D. doesn't matter where

6. When riding your bike, how should you notify others that you will be turning?

    _____

Subtract to solve each problem. Regroup if necessary.

1. 837
    − 138

2. 516
    − 247

3. 825
    − 356

4. 713
    − 284

5. 624
    − 367

6. 283
    − 96

7. 567
    − 275

8. 928
    − 189

9. 785
    − 496

10. 497
    − 269

11. 553
    − 129

12. 476
    − 138

13. 764
    − 335

14. 676
    − 227

15. 952
    − 344

16. 837
    − 253

17. 689
    − 496

18. 941
    − 250

19. 277
    − 193

20. 765
    − 295

Boredom Busters

Feeling bored this summer? Instead of complaining or moping, here's another solution: Make a Boredom Buster list for those times when it seems like there's nothing to do. First, pick a letter of the alphabet. Then, list ten things you wish you were doing that start with that letter. Finally, pick the best thing on the list and do it. Save your list for the next time you are bored or make a new one with a new letter.

Write the word *went* or *gone* to complete each sentence. Remember: The word *gone* needs another word to help it, such as *has* or *have*.

1. Carlos _____ to the park after school.

2. Kami has _____ shopping for new shoes.

3. Ebony _____ with Byron to play.

4. We will be _____ on vacation all week.

5. My father _____ to work this evening.

Write a word from each box to complete each sentence.

6. The car will _____ .

   The car is _____ .

   The car has _____ .

> **stop**
> **stopped**
> **stopping**

7. The baby can _____ .

   The baby is _____ .

   The baby _____ .

> **crawl**
> **crawled**
> **crawling**

8. The kangaroo is _____ .

   The kangaroo _____ .

   The kangaroo can _____ .

> **hop**
> **hopped**
> **hopping**

Use a ruler to measure the length of each fish.

1.

_____ in.

2.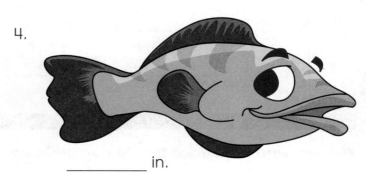

_____ in.

3.

_____ in.

4.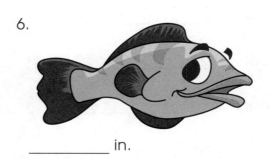

_____ in.

5.

_____ in.

6.

_____ in.

Use the information above to fill in the line plot.

Fish in the Pond

$2\frac{1}{4}$ $2\frac{1}{2}$ $2\frac{3}{4}$ 3 $3\frac{1}{4}$

Write the best adjective from the word bank to complete each sentence.

rainy	equal	low	little

1. I put an _____ amount of ice cream in my bowl and yours.

2. There is a _____ bug on the window.

3. Monica stepped over the _____ wall.

4. She saw a rainbow in the sky on the _____ day.

Circle and write the correct contraction to complete each sentence.
EXAMPLE:

_____They've_____ never played baseball.

They're   **They'll**   (**They've**)

5. _____ have a really exciting time.

   We're   **We'll**   **We've**

6. _____ going to see a play tomorrow.

   We'll   **We're**   **We've**

7. _____ work as fast as I can.

   I'm   **I've**   **I'll**

8. _____ got to do it right the first time.

   We've   **We'll**   **We're**

Animals Abound

Read the poem.

How many animals can you name?
This seems like a never-ending game.

There are little ants so very small.
There are spotted giraffes so very tall.

There are mammals and insects to name a few.
There are reptiles and amphibians in the zoo.

There are animals that fly and some that walk.
There are cows in a herd and birds in a flock.

There are animals on land and at sea.
There are animals in the ground and some in trees.

There are animals that are wild and some that are tame.
There are too many animals to ever name!

Use the poem to answer the questions.

1. What is the main idea of the poem?
   A. There are too many animals to name.
   B. Animals make great pets.
   C. Some animals are wild, and some are tame.

2. Three animals that are mentioned by name in the poem are
   A. giraffes, ants, and cows.
   B. sea animals, cows, and ants.
   C. sea turtles, crows, and ants.

3. Draw a line between antonyms.

land	tame
ground	sky
wild	tall
few	sea
small	many

4. Find five plural nouns in the poem. Write them on the lines.

   _____

   _____

   _____

5. Cross out the animal that does not belong in each group.

A. hawk	owl	whale	robin
B. horse	cow	sheep	giraffe
C. squirrel	monkey	dog	koala
D. snake	ant	cricket	grasshopper
E. tiger	lion	rabbit	leopard

Add or subtract to solve each problem.

1. Anthony had 348 pennies. His brother had 239. How many more pennies did Anthony have than his brother?

2. Celeste collected 479 aluminum cans. Nicole collected 742 cans. How many cans did the girls collect altogether?

3. The electronics store had 371 televisions in stock. They sold 138 on the weekend. How many televisions do they have left?

4. My big brother Matt weighs 189 pounds. His friend weighs 202 pounds. How much less does Matt weigh than his friend?

5. The school library has 879 nonfiction books and 932 fiction books. How many books does the library have altogether?

6. The girls earned 487 points for selling cookies. The boys earned 399 points. How many more points did the girls earn than the boys?

CHARACTER CHECK: What does it mean to show good sportsmanship? What are some ways you can be a good sport while playing games with your friends?

Complete the fractions. The first one is done for you.

1. $= \dfrac{2}{2}$

2.  $= \underline{\hspace{2cm}}$

3.  $= \underline{\hspace{2cm}}$

4. $= \underline{\hspace{2cm}}$

5.  $= \underline{\hspace{2cm}}$

6. $= \underline{\hspace{2cm}}$

7. $= \underline{\hspace{2cm}}$

8. 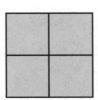 $= \underline{\hspace{2cm}}$

Circle the adjectives that describe each underlined noun.

1. I have a green and red <u>jacket</u>.

2. The little yellow <u>snake</u> climbed the tree.

3. Uma made a costume from colorful, soft <u>cloth</u>.

4. The dark gray <u>cloud</u> is over my house.

5. I wore new gray <u>boots</u> today.

Write the two words that make each contraction.
EXAMPLE:

hasn't _____**has not**_____

6. I'm _____

7. you'll _____

8. didn't _____

9. she'd _____

10. we'd _____

11. you're _____

12. he's _____

13. won't _____

14. I'll _____

15. we'll _____

16. they're _____

Draw the hands on each clock to show the time.

1.

8:35

2.

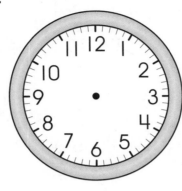

9:50

3.

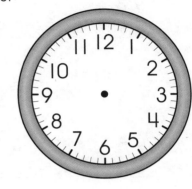

6:47

4.

12:23

5.

10:25

6.

7:53

7.

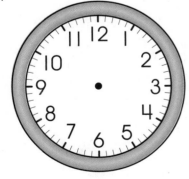

11:08

8.

4:47

9.

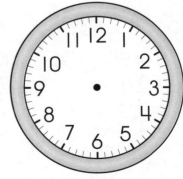

6:17

Add or subtract to solve each problem. Regroup if necessary.

1. 93
    + 29

2. 86
    + 93

3. 132
    − 41

4. 186
    − 92

5.   76
    + 192

6. 145
    − 82

7. 543
    − 206

8. 150
    − 90

9. 173
    + 420

10. 159
    − 82

11. 158
    − 69

12. 432
    − 257

13. 415
    + 826

14. 432
    − 119

15. 720
    + 140

16. 168
    − 109

17. 821
    + 39

18. 712
    − 347

19. 690
    − 320

20. 451
    − 253

21. 119
    + 104

22. 307
    + 291

23. 618
    − 127

24. 186
    + 210

25. 932
    − 721

FACTOID: Ostriches can run faster than horses.

Write an adjective to complete each sentence.

1. Hector showed me the _____ picture.

2. The _____ puppy is chasing his tail.

3. That _____ bird flies south for the winter.

4. Tony carried the _____ bag.

5. That binder with the _____ cover is mine.

Important words in titles begin with capital letters. Look for the title in each sentence. Mark the letters that should be capitalized. Use this proofreading symbol: m̲.

6. Quinn's favorite book is *charlie and the chocolate factory*.

7. Have you ever seen the movie *stuart little*?

8. When Mom was little, she loved to watch *mister rogers' neighborhood*.

9. Kevin knows all the words to his favorite song, "Don't worry, be happy."

10. Last weekend, we rented the movie *How to train your dragon*.

11. Grandma used to sing Darius to sleep by singing "walking after midnight."

12. Did you read *the hobbit* before seeing the movie?

CHARACTER CHECK: Who has been generous to you? How can you be generous to someone else?

Write an addition and multiplication problem for each picture. Then, find the sum and the product.

1.
× × × × ×
× × × × ×
× × × × ×

2 + 2 + 1 = ☐

☐ × ☐ = ☐

2.
☆ ☆ ☆
☆ ☆ ☆

☐ + ☐ = ☐

☐ × ☐ = ☐

3.
● ●
● ●
● ●
● ●

☐ + ☐ + ☐ + ☐ = ☐

☐ × ☐ = ☐

4.
ⓒ ⓒ ⓒ ⓒ
ⓒ ⓒ ⓒ ⓒ

☐ + ☐ = ☐

☐ × ☐ = ☐

5.
× × ×
× × ×
× × ×

☐ + ☐ + ☐ = ☐

☐ × ☐ = ☐

6.
★ ★ ★ ★
★ ★ ★ ★
★ ★ ★ ★

☐ + ☐ + ☐ = ☐

☐ × ☐ = ☐

7.
● ●
● ●
● ●

☐ + ☐ + ☐ = ☐

☐ × ☐ = ☐

8.
ⓒ ⓒ ⓒ ⓒ ⓒ
ⓒ ⓒ ⓒ ⓒ ⓒ

☐ + ☐ = ☐

☐ × ☐ = ☐

FITNESS FLASH: Sit with your legs apart. Bend slowly over your right leg (no bouncing!) and hold the position for 10 seconds. Then do the same over the middle and over your left leg.

Write the two words that make each contraction.

1. he's _____

2. she's _____

3. aren't _____

4. they've _____

5. I've _____

6. I'd _____

7. it's _____

8. didn't _____

9. she'll _____

10. shouldn't _____

11. he'll _____

12. we'd _____

Abstract nouns name feelings, concepts, and ideas. Some examples are *hope*, *bravery*, and *pride*. Underline the abstract noun in each sentence.

13. Mr. and Mrs. Kim were filled with pride when Irene won the geography bee.

14. Dad always talks about the adventurous childhood he had with his brothers.

15. My favorite thing about Mario is his generosity.

16. Drew could see the delight on Megan's face as she opened her gift.

17. "I really appreciate your honesty," said Principal Conti.

18. I can count on Norris to always tell me the truth.

Solve the problems.

1. The town of Norwood is planning a skateboard park and needs to know the perimeter of the park. The property measures 7 yards by 3 yards by 10 yards by 5 yards. What is the perimeter?

   The park's perimeter is _____ yards.

2. Kenyon cleared a vacant lot to plant flowers. The lot measured 35 by 15 feet. What is the perimeter of the lot?

   The perimeter of the lot is _____ feet.

3. Frederico built a cage for his carrier pigeons. The cage measures 15 feet by 13 feet. What is the perimeter of the cage?

   The perimeter of the cage is _____ feet.

4. The length of the running track is 103 feet and the width is 50 feet. What is the perimeter of the track?

   The perimeter is _____ feet.

5. Beth is buying trim to go around her rug. Her rug measures 54 inches by 42 inches. How many inches of trim will Beth need to buy?

   Beth will need to buy _____ inches of trim.

6. Melinda is putting stones around her fish pond. Her pond is 10 feet by 8 feet. How many feet of stone trim will Melinda need?

   Melinda will need _____ feet of stone trim.

7. The rectangular third-grade classroom has a perimeter of 130 feet. If it is 25 feet wide, how many feet long is the classroom?

   The classroom is _____ feet long.

Multiplication

Complete the multiplication chart. Then, answer the questions.

X	1	2	3	4	5	6	7	8	9
1									
2									
3									
4									
5									
6									
7									
8									
9									

1. What does any number times 1 equal?_____

2. What pattern do you see in the twos? _____

_____

3. What pattern do you see in the fives?_____

_____

4. Add the digits for each answer in the nines. What number does each answer

   equal? _____

5. 3 x 4 = 12. What does 4 x 3 equal? _____

Dear Donna

Read the letter. Then, answer the questions on the next page.

June 13, 2014

Dear Donna,

The other day was a bad day for my mom and me. I forgot to pick a few ears of corn from our garden for dinner, and she was upset. She even *restricted* me to my room so I couldn't play outside. I can understand why she was so upset with me; I forgot to do my chores.

A few hours after she sent me to my room, I apologized to her for forgetting. I think my apology made my mom feel better, because she let me go outside to play. I was excited to use the new kite that I got for my birthday.

The sun was shining brightly, and there was just enough wind to fly my kite. After I looked at the kite flying high up in the sky, a feeling of happiness came over me. It was like magic!

The wind started to die down, so I decided to pull my kite down and go home. The minute I walked into the kitchen holding my kite, my mom smiled at me. I asked her why she was smiling. Mom told me that my red cheeks and the smile on my face made her happy!

After dinner, I went to my mom and kissed her on the cheek. She asked me why I did that. I told her that her smile made me happy. It was a good ending to a bad day. I hope to hear from you soon.

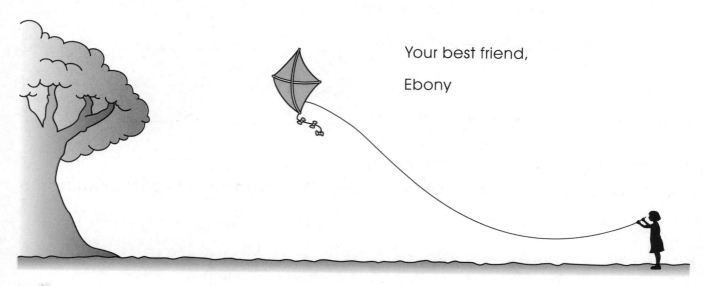

Your best friend,

Ebony

Use the letter to answer the questions.

1. The word *restricted* means

   A. tricked again   B. kept within limits

   C. yelled   D. upset

2. What was Ebony's punishment for not completing her chore?

   A. cleaning her room   B. flying a kite

   C. not playing outside   D. cleaning the dishes

3. What feeling did Ebony get when she was able to fly her kite?

   A. happy   B. depressed

   C. anxious   D. scared

4. What made Ebony's mother happy?

   A. dinner   B. Ebony's red cheeks and smile

   C. Ebony's kite   D. gardening

5. Why do you think Ebony likes to see her mother smile?

   _____

   _____

   _____

   _____

   _____

Find the product for each pair of factors below. Use the code to find the letters. Write the letters on the lines to answer the two riddles.

A	B	C	D	E	F	G	H	I	J	K	L	M	N	O	P	Q	R	S	T	U	V	W	X	Y	Z
64	4	42	27	24	16	0	18	40	11	19	49	59	25	12	13	21	56	8	54	32	28	45	60	9	14

How do you make the number *one* disappear?

___ ___ ___   ___ ___ ___
8 × 8   9 × 3   3 × 9   9 × 6   2 × 9   3 × 8

___ ___ ___ ___ ___ ___   ___
7 × 7   6 × 4   6 × 9   9 × 6   8 × 3   7 × 8   10 × 0

,

___ ___ ___   ___ ___ ___
8 × 8   5 × 5   9 × 3   8 × 5   9 × 6   4 × 2

"___ ___ ___ ___"!
8 × 0   3 × 4   5 × 5   4 × 6

What can you hold in your left hand but not in your right hand?

___ ___ ___ ___
3 × 3   6 × 2   8 × 4   7 × 8

___ ___ ___ ___ ___
8 × 7   5 × 8   1 × 0   6 × 3   6 × 9

___ ___ ___ ___ ___!
8 × 3   7 × 7   2 × 2   3 × 4   9 × 5

Take a Trip, Final Step

Now that you are back from your imaginary trip, you are ready to make a journal that shows all the places you visited!

What you'll need:

- the map of your trip
- sheets of paper
- glue or tape
- markers, colored pencils, or crayons
- stapler

What to do:

1. Think about each place you visited. How did you get there? What sights and attractions did you see while you were there? What did you have to eat? Where did you stay?
2. Plan at least a page for each place you visited. You can make more than one page if you like. At the top of the page, write the name of the place you visited. Underneath, write about all the things you saw and did there. Make sure to leave room on each page for pictures!
3. Illustrate each page with drawings of the place you visited. Or, you could print out photos from the Internet, cut them out, and glue them to the page.
4. Include the map you drew as one of the pages in your journal. You can put it in the front or the back, or in the middle.
5. Make a cover page for your journal. It should include a picture of your favorite place from the trip. Write a title for your journal, too.
6. Staple your journal pages and cover together. If you need help, ask an adult.

Have fun putting together your journal! Here is one way you could design a page:

Here is one way you could make a cover for your journal:

Chicago

July 10

Today I flew in a jetliner to Chicago, Illinois. After I arrived, I took a trip to the Willis Tower. It is the second-tallest building in the United States. You can see a long way when you are at the top! For lunch, I had a slice of deep-dish pizza with mushrooms and sausage. Chicago is famous for its deep-dish pizza.

Emma's Summer Travel Journal

Someone Else's Shoes, Final Step

Now you are ready to write a movie scene starring your character. Your scene could be an adventure, a conversation, a funny situation, or a problem your character has to solve. Use your imagination!

What to do:

1. Think about the questions you answered in Step 3. What kind of situations, problems, or adventures would your animal or insect character face in its life? How would it respond?

2. Choose what you want your scene to be about. Will your character be alone, or will other characters be involved?

3. Think about how to tell the story and show the action in your scene. What will your character do? What will it say?

4. On a separate piece of paper, write down what your character will do and say. Write down what any other characters in the scene will do and say. Look at the next page for an example of how to write your scene.

Now that you have written a scene for your character, it's time to perform it!

What to do:

1. If your scene has more than one character, ask your friends or family members to help. Make sure to give them a copy of the scene you wrote so they can learn their parts.

2. Make costumes for your animal or insect character and any other characters in the scene.

3. Find a place to perform your scene. Make sure you have enough room for all the characters and actions you included.

4. Practice acting out your scene. Does the story make sense? Do you need to add anything or take anything out?

5. Invite friends and family to watch you perform your scene! You could even record the performance and send a link to out-of-town friends and family as well.

Movie Scene Example
Saved by a Splash

Characters:
Tipsy the Flamingo
Tipsy's sister, Pinky

Scene: An island in the Caribbean Sea

[Tipsy the Flamingo stands in the water on one leg, sleeping. Nearby, his sister Pinky is also sleeping on one leg. Suddenly, Tipsy falls over with a big SPLASH!]

Pinky: Honk! Honk! What was that?

Tipsy (picking himself up out of the water)**:** I fell over again in my sleep. This is so embarrassing! All the other flamingos can stand on one leg and sleep. Why can't I do it, too?

Pinky (annoyed)**:** I don't know, but I'm really tired of you falling over and waking me up every night!

Tipsy (hangs head)**:** I'm sorry, Pinky. Please don't be mad. I'll go off and sleep someplace where I won't wake anybody up.

[Pinky starts to answer, but another splash interrupts her.]

Tipsy: Pinky, look out! A crocodile!

[The crocodile lunges at Tipsy and Pinky, but it is too slow. The flamingos soar into the air and fly away.]

Pinky: That was scary! We were almost a crocodile's midnight snack. Tipsy, I'm sorry I got mad at you for waking me up. If you hadn't fallen over, we'd still be asleep and the croc would have eaten us!

Tipsy: Wow, you're right. Maybe I'm not such a flamingo failure after all!

Adopt an Animal

The seas of the world are filled with an amazing variety of life. Starfish, crabs, flying fish, angelfish, worms, turtles, sharks and whales all make their homes underwater. The shape, color, and size of most sea animals depend on their lifestyles and where they live in the seas. Select a sea animal and become an expert on it. Research your animal and complete the profile below.

Common Name_____

Scientific Name _____

Description:

weight:

length:

body shape:

tail shape:

color:

unusual characteristics:

Picture

Behaviors

Description of Habitat: _____

_____

Food and Feeding Habits: _____

_____

_____

Migration (if applicable): _____

_____

_____

In the Water

Much of Earth is covered with water. Try the following activity to examine some properties of water.

What you'll need:
- several objects that will react differently when put into a basin of water (i.e., a block of wood, a paper clip, a pencil, sugar, salt, a sponge, a piece of fabric, a rubber band, an eraser, baking soda, a paper towel, a nail, etc.
- a large basin of water
- the chart below

Predict what will happen to each object when it is put into a basin of water. Record this information on the chart. Conduct the experiments and record what actually happened. Compare your predictions with the actual results.

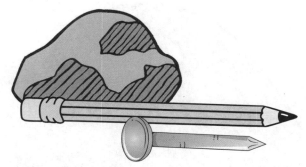

Object/Item	Predictions of what will happen	Results of what happened

BONUS

Take It Outside!

Cool off from your summer adventures with water tag. Give a cup of water to one friend, who is "it." Fill a large bucket to be home base. When you say go, "it" should run around and try to tag someone with water. She can refill as often as she likes. The first person to be soaked is the next "it."

Veins help move blood around your body. Leaves have veins, too. Use a magnifying glass to examine a few leaves. Find the largest vein down the middle and then look for smaller veins. Which leaf has the most veins?

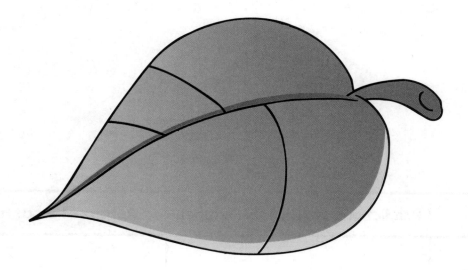

Draw a line down the middle of a piece of paper. On one side, write "Natural." On the other side, write "Manmade." Look up at the sky. Write down everything you see that is part of nature under the natural column. Write everything that is manmade in the manmade column.

Section III Introduction

Theme: My Summer Adventures

This month's explorations invite your child to reflect on her experiences as the end of summer vacation approaches. They encourage her to use her growing skills to tell her own stories in imaginative ways. Before the beginning of a new school year, take the time to talk with your child about how much she has grown and changed. Measure and record her height and weight and look back at old photos together. Ask her to show off how good she is at swimming, playing sports, reading and writing words, doing math problems, and other skills that show her growing maturity. Make sure to ask what she is looking forward to learning in the new school year.

To build language arts and literacy skills this month, visit the library and challenge your child to choose a book that is a little longer or more difficult than what he is used to. Encourage him to begin a list of new vocabulary words he is learning from his reading that he can begin to build on throughout the school year. Take advantage of back-to-school sales and purchase supplies for a home writing center. These can include pencils, pens, markers, envelopes, notebooks, index cards, and stickers. Encourage your child to write letters and stories for fun every day.

To build math skills this month, familiarize your child with basic multiplication and division facts using dice, dominoes, or everyday household items. Challenge her to think about simple fractions at the dinner table. For example, if a pizza is cut into eight slices and the child eats two of them, what share of the pizza did she eat?

Explorations

This month, your child will have a choice of two explorations. He may choose to follow steps for one or both. Review the explorations below with your child and help him make a choice. Emphasize that it is useful to have a path in mind from the start. Then, help your child find and complete the project activities according to his plan. Throughout the section, your child will see the icons shown below on pages that include directions directly related to one of the explorations. Emphasize that breaking a large project into smaller steps helps make it fun and easy to do.

 Guide to Summer Fun

With this exploration, your child will develop language arts, writing, and communication skills by creating a guidebook that provides information about her favorite summer activities. She will collect, organize, and recount details of her most enjoyable adventures, writing informative instructions and persuasive descriptions so readers of her guidebook can enjoy the adventures, too.

To help your child complete this exploration, prompt her to recount her favorite summer adventures to you. Challenge her to persuade you to try them. Identify some of your child's most effective descriptions and encourage her to elaborate on them for her guidebook. Finally, ask her if there are any summer activities she wants to do but hasn't been able to yet. Offer guidance on how she can still complete them—and include them in her guidebook!—before school starts again.

 The Game of Summer

With this exploration, your child will hone his creative thinking, writing, and communication skills by developing a board game based on summer activities. His creative thinking skills will come into play as he designs a game board, comes up with fun game pieces, creates effective game elements, and tests the game by playing it. His writing skills will be stretched as he develops clear rules and instructions for how to play. And he will practice communication skills as he explains the game to new players and incorporates their feedback to make the game even better.

To help your child with this exploration, play some of your favorite board games together. Ask him to identify what he likes the most about them, and challenge him to include some of those elements in his own game. Once your child has designed his game, offer your services as a game tester. Play it with him and offer suggestions and feedback. Are the rules clear and easy to follow?

Learning Activities

Practice pages for this month introduce skills your child will learn in the third grade. They also focus on skills that support the explorations described above. Preview the activities and choose several that target skills your child needs to practice. Also select several relating to the exploration(s) your child plans to complete. You may wish to mark those pages with a star or other symbol to let your child know to begin with those. Then, let your child choose practice activities that interest her and allow her to demonstrate her growing skills.

Guide to Summer Fun, Step 1

It's almost time to go back to school. But, with this exploration, you can relive all the adventures you had during your break by creating a guidebook to summer fun!

First, think about all the fun things you have done this summer. Did you go camping or spend a day at the beach with your family? Did you play any outdoor sports with your friends? Did you attend a baseball game or visit an amusement park? Make a list of all your adventures. Are there any other activities you would like to do before back-to-school? Put those on the list, too, and see if you can make them happen.

Summer Fun

1. _____
2. _____
3. _____
4. _____
5. _____
6. _____
7. _____
8. _____
9. _____
10. _____
11. _____
12. _____

The Game of Summer, Step I

In this exploration, you will design your own board game based on summer activities!

First, consider everything you like about summer as well as any plans you have. Your game could focus on one event or you could incorporate all that you plan to do or wish you could do this summer. You decide!

Here are a few ideas to get you started:

- A board game where each player tries to advance along the board while completing summer activities. The first one to the end or first one to complete them all wins.
- A board game based on summer fun spots in your neighborhood. Players move through or capture locations like swimming pools, soccer fields, community centers, and ice cream stores.
- A board game focused on your favorite summer activity or sport, like playing basketball or visiting amusement parks.

Which summer activity or activities will your game focus on?

_____

_____

_____

_____

_____

_____

_____

_____

_____

_____

_____

Take It Outside!

Write each letter of the alphabet on an index card. Go outside with the cards. Look for something that starts with *A*, such as an acorn. Write acorn on the *A* card. Keep going until you find something for every letter. Look out—some are tricky!

After it rains, draw a chalk line around a puddle on the sidewalk. For the next few days, draw a line around the puddle at the same time each day. What do you notice about the puddle each day? What is happening to it?

Some say that fireflies light up to meet other fireflies. Sit outside in a grassy area at dusk. Count the number of fireflies you see for two minutes and write the number down. Turn on a small flashlight. Then, count fireflies for two more minutes and write that number down. Did you see more or fewer fireflies with the flashlight on?

What fraction of each figure is shaded? Compare the fractions. Use >, <, or =.

1.

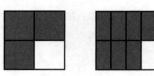

_____ ◯ _____

2.

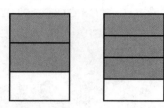

_____ ◯ _____

3.

_____ ◯ _____

4.

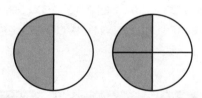

◯

_____ _____

5.

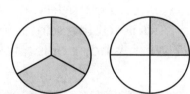

◯

_____ _____

6.

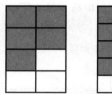

◯

_____ _____

7.

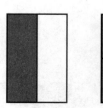

◯

_____ _____

8.

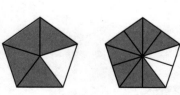

◯

_____ _____

9.

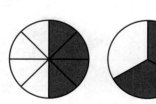

◯

_____ _____

Underline the verb that completes each sentence.

1. Colby and Zoe (are, is) going on a spring scavenger hunt.

2. Colby (spot, spots) leaves budding on a tree.

3. Zoe (see, sees) a robin searching for worms in the green grass.

4. A warm breeze (melt, melts) the last of the snow.

5. A kite (soar, soars) overhead.

6. Daffodils and tulips (bloom, blooms) in the garden.

7. The children (hear, hears) happy songbirds singing.

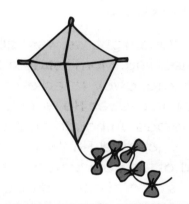

Use a conjunction from the word bank to complete each sentence. Do not use the same conjunction more than once.

and	although	while	but	or	because	until	whether

8. _____ Dad doesn't like coffee, he loves the way it smells.

9. Edgar took out the garbage, _____ Marisa cleared the table.

10. _____ the sun comes out or not, we will enjoy the party.

11. Nathan is almost a year old, _____ he is not walking yet.

12. Please don't open your gifts _____ your grandparents get here.

13. Sandra has to go to the doctor _____ she has an earache.

Stray Cat Hero

Read the story.

My mom always takes in stray animals. The one I remember best was a mangy kitten.

One day, a dirty, hungry little kitten wandered onto our porch. Mom took pity on the kitten. She brought it in the house, gave it a bath, and fed it. She took special care of this kitten.

One night, we were all sound asleep. At about two in the morning, I heard loud meowing. Mom's stray kitten jumped next to my face and began to lick me. I pushed the cat away, rolled over, and went back to sleep. The persistent cat wouldn't take no for an answer. He went to my dad. My dad pushed the cat over to my mom's side of the bed. Although my mom is a very heavy sleeper, the cat continued to meow and lick her face. Finally, my mom awoke. At first, she was annoyed. But, then she realized what the cat wanted. Mom smelled gas. She immediately woke Dad. They turned the gas off and opened all of the windows. We had a gas leak that no one noticed except our stray cat. Mom's stray cat had saved us. That's how the little stray kitten became our family pet, and that's how Hero got his name!

Use the story to answer the questions.

1. Number the sentences in the order that they happened in the story.

    _____ Mom took care of a stray cat.

    _____ We named the stray cat Hero.

    _____ The cat tried to wake Dad.

    _____ The cat woke Mom.

    _____ Mom smelled gas.

    _____ Mom and Dad turned off the gas.

2. Circle the correct answer.

    Because Hero woke Mom,
    A. she got scratched.
    B. she smelled the gas.
    C. the family awoke.

    They opened all of the windows
    A. to let Hero outside.
    B. because they were hot.
    C. because there was a gas smell.

    Mom gave the kitten a bath
    A. because no one else would.
    B. because it asked her to.
    C. because it was dirty and she felt pity for it.

3. Draw a line between the present tense and past tense of each word.

    take   brought
    become   went
    bring   began
    begin   took
    go   became

4. What is a stray animal?
    A. a dangerous animal
    B. a dirty animal
    C. an animal without a home

5. Someone who is persistent
    A. doesn't give up.
    B. is very loud.
    C. can smell very well.

6. Use the word *and* to combine the sentences below. Rewrite them on the lines.

    Our cat smelled gas. He tried to wake us.

    _____

    _____

    _____

    Mom takes in stray animals. She gives them baths.

    _____

    _____

    _____

Multiply to solve each problem.

1. $\begin{array}{r} 2 \\ \times\ 2 \\ \hline \end{array}$
2. $\begin{array}{r} 3 \\ \times\ 2 \\ \hline \end{array}$
3. $\begin{array}{r} 5 \\ \times\ 3 \\ \hline \end{array}$
4. $\begin{array}{r} 1 \\ \times\ 6 \\ \hline \end{array}$
5. $\begin{array}{r} 6 \\ \times\ 2 \\ \hline \end{array}$

6. $\begin{array}{r} 2 \\ \times\ 8 \\ \hline \end{array}$
7. $\begin{array}{r} 5 \\ \times\ 2 \\ \hline \end{array}$
8. $\begin{array}{r} 2 \\ \times\ 6 \\ \hline \end{array}$
9. $\begin{array}{r} 2 \\ \times\ 4 \\ \hline \end{array}$
10. $\begin{array}{r} 2 \\ \times\ 1 \\ \hline \end{array}$

11. $\begin{array}{r} 7 \\ \times\ 2 \\ \hline \end{array}$
12. $\begin{array}{r} 3 \\ \times\ 6 \\ \hline \end{array}$
13. $\begin{array}{r} 9 \\ \times\ 2 \\ \hline \end{array}$
14. $\begin{array}{r} 8 \\ \times\ 2 \\ \hline \end{array}$
15. $\begin{array}{r} 4 \\ \times\ 5 \\ \hline \end{array}$

16. $\begin{array}{r} 3 \\ \times\ 9 \\ \hline \end{array}$
17. $\begin{array}{r} 6 \\ \times\ 5 \\ \hline \end{array}$
18. $\begin{array}{r} 4 \\ \times\ 6 \\ \hline \end{array}$
19. $\begin{array}{r} 3 \\ \times\ 7 \\ \hline \end{array}$
20. $\begin{array}{r} 8 \\ \times\ 3 \\ \hline \end{array}$

21. $\begin{array}{r} 4 \\ \times\ 4 \\ \hline \end{array}$
22. $\begin{array}{r} 5 \\ \times\ 6 \\ \hline \end{array}$
23. $\begin{array}{r} 5 \\ \times\ 8 \\ \hline \end{array}$
24. $\begin{array}{r} 7 \\ \times\ 9 \\ \hline \end{array}$
25. $\begin{array}{r} 8 \\ \times\ 8 \\ \hline \end{array}$

26. $\begin{array}{r} 5 \\ \times\ 4 \\ \hline \end{array}$
27. $\begin{array}{r} 8 \\ \times\ 9 \\ \hline \end{array}$
28. $\begin{array}{r} 7 \\ \times\ 6 \\ \hline \end{array}$
29. $\begin{array}{r} 5 \\ \times\ 7 \\ \hline \end{array}$
30. $\begin{array}{r} 4 \\ \times\ 8 \\ \hline \end{array}$

Multiply to solve each problem.

1. Jason has 4 bags. He puts 5 marbles in each bag. How many marbles are there in all?

   Jason has _____ bags.

   Each bag has _____ marbles.

   There are _____ marbles in all.

2. There are 4 pots of flowers. There are 2 flowers in each pot. How many flowers are there in all?

   There are _____ pots.

   Each pot has _____ flowers.

   There are _____ flowers in all.

3. Kami jumped over 4 rocks. She jumped over each rock 3 times. How many times did she jump in all?

   There are _____ rocks.

   Kami jumped over each rock _____ times.

   She jumped _____ times in all.

Write a word problem to fit the number sentence. Solve.

5 x 1 = _____

_____

_____

_____

Add the ending shown to each base word to make a new word. Don't forget to change the spelling of the base word when the ending is added.

change _y_ to _i_

1. fly + s = _____

2. happy + ness _____

drop the final _e_

5. smile + ed = _____

6. pile + ing = _____

double the final consonant

3. sip + ing = _____

4. hop + ed = _____

change _ie_ to _y_ or _y_ to _ie_

7. lie + ing = _____

8. kitty + s = _____

Write _N_ if the verb is in the present tense (happening now). Write _P_ if the verb is in the past tense (already happened). Write _F_ if the verb is in the future tense (will happen in the future).

9. _____ We will run later.

10. _____ I have a sandwich.

11. _____ Hugo ate a cucumber.

12. _____ We will go home soon.

13. _____ I love cucumbers!

14. _____ Neyla is playing soccer.

15. _____ I biked with my mom.

16. _____ Jarvis washed his dog.

FACTOID: When howler monkeys howl, they can be heard from up to 3 miles away.

Geometry

Count the squares ☐ that make up each rectangle.

1.

_____ equal squares

2.

_____ equal squares

3.

_____ equal squares

Draw same-size squares ☐ to fill each rectangle. Then, count the number of squares.

4.

_____ square units

5.

_____ square units

6.

_____ square units

7.

_____ square units

8.

_____ square units

9.

_____ square units

Sea Horses

Read the passage.

Sea horses are interesting creatures for many reasons. Their scientific name is *Hippocampus*. It comes from two Greek words: *hippos*, which means "horse" and *kampos*, which means "sea monster." To survive in the ocean, sea horses live in environments that camouflage them from predators. Sea horses range in size from 6 to 12 inches, although most are about 6 inches long. They can be many colors, including white, yellow, red, brown, black, and gray, with spots or stripes. However, the most interesting thing about sea horses is that they put a twist on parenting. Instead of females carrying the young, males carry them!

A male sea horse has a pouch on his underside where he carries eggs. The female sea horse places her eggs into the male's pouch. Then, the male sea horse carries the eggs for about 21 days until they hatch. The female sea horse visits the male sea horse every morning until the babies are born. Newborn sea horses rise to the surface of the water and take a gulp of air, which helps them stay upright.

When sea horses are born, they feed on tiny sea creatures, using their snouts. They are able to swim, but sometimes they get washed up onshore by storms or eaten by fish, crabs, or water birds.

A few days after giving birth, the male joins the female again. Within hours, he has a new sack full of eggs. This is the life cycle of the sea horse. Sea horses are indeed interesting animals!

Use the passage to answer the questions.

1. What do newborn sea horses usually eat?

   A. crabs

   B. flowers

   C. tiny sea animals

   D. sand

2. What does it mean to "put a twist on" something?

   _____

   _____

3. Why do newborn sea horses rise to the surface of the water?

   _____

   _____

4. What word means "sea monster"?

   A. kampos

   B. phylum

   C. hippos

   D. genus

5. In your opinion, what is the most interesting thing about the sea horse?

   _____

   _____

   _____

   _____

CHARACTER CHECK: What do you complain about the most? What could you do about it instead of complaining?

Multiply to solve each problem.

1. Tripp wants to buy 6 pieces of bubblegum. Each
   piece costs 5 cents. How much will he have to pay
   for the bubblegum?

   Tripp wants to buy _____ pieces of bubblegum.

   One piece of bubblegum costs _____ cents.

   Tripp will have to pay _____ cents total.

2. There are 7 girls on stage. Each girl is holding 8 flowers. How many flowers are
   there in all?

   There are _____ girls.

   Each girl is holding _____ flowers.

   There are _____ flowers in all.

3. There are 3 rows of desks. There are 8 desks in each row. How many desks are
   there in all?

   There are _____ rows of desks.

   There are _____ desks in each row.

   There are _____ desks in all.

Write a word problem to fit the number sentence. Solve.

$8 \times 4 =$ _____

_____

_____

_____

Read each scale. Write the measurement. Circle the best unit of measurement by using the weight chart below.

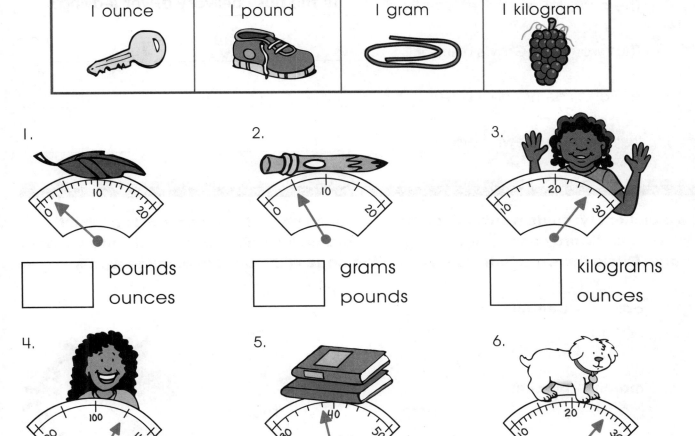

I ounce	I pound	I gram	I kilogram

1.

☐ pounds
ounces

2.

☐ grams
pounds

3.

☐ kilograms
ounces

4.

☐ grams
pounds

5.

☐ pounds
ounces

6.

☐ grams
pounds

FITNESS FLASH: Stretch a long piece of string in a straight line on the floor. Slowly walk heel-to-toe along the string. How far can you walk the "tightrope" without falling off?

Change each declarative sentence into an interrogative sentence.
EXAMPLE:

The busy delivery driver is leaving.   **Is the busy delivery driver leaving?**

1. That woman is Grey's mother. _____

2. She can ride her new bike. _____

3. I will ride the brown horse. _____

In a dictionary, guide words are at the top of each page. The guide word on the left tells the first word on the page. The guide word on the right tells the last word on the page. Circle the word that would be on the page with each set of guide words.

4. **pastor — penguin**
    panda   pig   paw

5. **match — monkey**
    math   magic   moss

6. **bean — buffalo**
    butter   bag   bison

7. **hammer — hark**
    hall   hand   hail

8. **rabbit — rack**
    racer   racket   radius

Make a mental computation first. Then, solve the problem.

1. Eight girls and 5 boys each have a button collection. Each girl has 8 buttons in her collection, and each boy has 4 buttons in his collection. How many buttons altogether do the boys and girls have?

   Mental Computation: _____

   The boys and girls have _____ buttons altogether.

2. There are 3 rows of 5 computers in each office. If there are 6 offices in the building, how many computers are in the building altogether?

   Mental Computation: _____

   There are _____ computers in the building.

3. Lucy bought 5 bags of dried mango slices. Each bag has 7 slices. How many mango slices does Lucy have left over after she gives away 10 slices?

   Mental Computation: _____

   Lucy has _____ mango slices left.

4. Ishmael bought 6 boxes of Mighty Mints and 5 boxes of Fudge Crunchies. Each Mighty Mints box has 10 cookies and each Fudge Crunchies box has 7. How many cookies does Ishmael have altogether?

   Mental Computation: _____

   Ishmael has _____ cookies altogether.

FITNESS FLASH: Lie on your back. With your knees bent, raise your legs and pump them back and forth like you are riding a bicycle. Do this for 60 seconds.

Guide to Summer Fun, Step 2

Now that you have put together a list of all your summer adventures, it's time to start brainstorming ideas for your guide to summer fun!

What you'll need:
- sheets of paper
- markers, colored pencils, or crayons

What to do:

1. Take another look at your list on page 145. Cross off anything that did not happen this summer.

2. Use separate sheets of paper to make notes, draw pictures, and write down ideas about the activities on your list.

3. Think about what makes each adventure on your list so exciting and fun. What will make your readers want to try these activities, too?

4. Note details for each activity that will help your readers enjoy them, too. For example, if you went camping, you might want to include pictures that show how to set up a tent, instructions on how to safely toast marshmallows, and a list of equipment to pack. If you visited an amusement park, you might want to include drawings of your favorite rides, information on when the park opens and how much it costs to get in, and tips for avoiding long lines.

FACTOID: The Kingda Ka roller coaster at Six Flags in New Jersey has a height of 456 feet and speeds of up to 128 miles per hour!

Body Building Blocks

Just like some houses are built with bricks, your body is built with cells. Every part of your body is made of cells.

Cells differ in **size** and **shape**, but they all have a few things in common. All cells have a nucleus. The **nucleus** is the center of the cell. It controls the cell's activities.

Cells can **divide** and become two cells exactly like the original cell.

Your body has many kinds of cells. Each kind has a special job. **Muscle** cells help you move. **Nerve** cells carry messages between your brain and other parts of your body. Blood cells carry **oxygen** to other cells in your body.

Directions: Complete each sentence using the words in bold from above.

1. The ___ ___ ___ ___ ___ ___ ___ controls the cell's activities.
        3

    muscle cell

2. Cells differ in ___ ___ ___ ___ and ___ ___ ___ ___ ___.
                    2   **1**

3. One cell can ___ ___ ___ ___ ___ ___ into two cells.   **nerve cell**
                              6

4. ___ ___ ___ ___ ___ ___ cells help you move.
              5

    nucleus

5. Blood cells carry ___ ___ ___ ___ ___ ___ to other cells in your body.
                            4

Unscramble the numbered letters above to discover this amazing fact.

6. You began life as a ___ ___ ___ ___ ___ ___ cell!
                         1   2   3   4   5   6

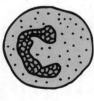

blood cells

BONUS

North, South, East, and West

You are flying in an airplane with the wind blowing sharply in your face. You are flying from Chicago to Nashville. In what direction are you traveling?

If you said "south" to the above question, you are correct!

Write the direction you would be traveling for each set of cities. Use the four cardinal directions—north, south, east and west.

Atlanta to Los Angeles _____

Seattle to Los Angeles _____

San Francisco to Nashville _____

Denver to Salt Lake City _____

Cincinnati to Detroit _____

Chicago to Boston _____

Houston to Minneapolis _____

Miami to New York _____

Detroit to New York _____

Boston to Minneapolis _____

Atlanta to Albuquerque _____

Nashville to Miami _____

Take It Outside!

Find a small hill outside. How many ways can you get down the hill? Try rolling, skipping, walking sideways, and more. When you cannot think of another way to get down the hill, try using each of those ways to get back up the hill. Which ways work better for going down, and which work better for going up?

Are ladybugs the same on both sides? Study a ladybug closely with a magnifying glass. Count the number of spots on each side. Does each side have the same number of spots? Are they in the same place? Find two more ladybugs. Are their spots the same as the first one's?

Go trail blazing. Cut a piece of colorful fabric into strips. As you take a walk, tie the strips to branches, signposts, or fences. Make sure you can still see the last strip as you tie a new one. Take a friend on a walk, and see if he or she can follow the trail. At the end of your walk, have your friend blaze a new trail for you to follow. When you finish, carefully remove all the fabric strips and take them home.

Circle equal groups to find the quotient for each picture.

1.

$10 \div 5 = \boxed{}$

2.

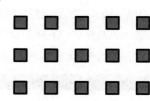

$15 \div 3 = \boxed{}$

3.

$6 \div 3 = \boxed{}$

4.

@ @ @ @

@ @ @ @

$8 \div 2 = \boxed{}$

5.

$9 \div 3 = \boxed{}$

6.

$12 \div 4 = \boxed{}$

7.

$12 \div 6 = \boxed{}$

8.

$18 \div 3 = \boxed{}$

9.

$14 \div 7 = \boxed{}$

CHARACTER CHECK: If someone gave you $20, would you save the money, spend it, or give it away?

An exclamatory sentence shows strong emotions or feelings. Write *E* for each exclamatory sentence. Write *D* for each declarative sentence. Write *I* for each interrogative sentence.

1. _____ What did he do?

2. _____ I am so happy for you!

3. _____ It's a girl!

4. _____ That is terrible news!

5. _____ The bird is red.

6. _____ Can I borrow a crayon?

Write each exclamatory sentence with a capital letter and an exclamation point (!).

7. look out _____

8. i had an amazing day _____

Write the missing comparative adjectives.

9. slow _____ _____

10. _____ _____ tallest

11. _____ warmer _____

12. bright _____ brightest

13. _____ higher _____

14. kind _____ _____

Eight Minutes Over France

Read the passage.

Do you like to travel in different ways? Then try going by hot air balloon. The idea had existed for 2,000 years. But, it took the king of France, two brothers, a sheep, a duck, and a chicken to make it happen.

The king of France thought a person would die traveling by balloon. So, two brothers did a test. They sent the three animals up in a basket attached to a balloon.

The animals flew over France for eight minutes. The king was excited when they returned safely. Two months later, a major in the army and a physics professor went up in a balloon.

A hot air balloon is so simple, anyone could fly one. Turning a knob lets gas into the balloon. This makes the balloon go up. Pulling a cord changes the amount of gas and makes the balloon rise quickly or slowly. If the cord lets enough gas out, the balloon sinks. The wind moves the balloon from place to place.

In the 1960s, hot air balloons became very popular. A man named Ed Yost worked with Raven Industries to design and make hot air balloons. Then, the United States Navy asked Ed's company to help them. The Navy wanted to use balloons to send packages.

Ed Yost and the Navy made important changes. Balloons were made from a new material. The balloon's shape was made to look like a giant light bulb.

Someone also invented a new way to inflate the balloon. Now just the top part of the balloon is filled. Some safety changes were also made. It is safer than ever to travel by hot air balloon.

After a while, the Navy lost interest in hot air balloons. But Ed Yost didn't give up. He sold hot air balloons for sporting events.

Hot air balloon businesses make millions of dollars. Balloon races attract crowds of watchers. Many people take part in the fun.

Use the passage to answer the questions.

1. If something can be proven or observed, it is a fact. If something can't be proven or observed, it is an opinion. Circle *F* for fact or *O* for opinion.

    The animals flew over France for eight minutes.   F   O

    A hot air balloon is so simple, anyone can fly one.   F   O

    It is safer than ever to travel by hot air balloon.   F   O

2. You can often guess what a word means by looking at the words around it. Review the passage and circle each correct answer.

    In the fourth paragraph, the word *sink* means
    A.   to go toward the ground.
    B.   to rise up slowly.
    C.   a place to wash your hands.

    The word *inflate* means
    A.   a new idea.
    B.   to fill something with air.
    C.   a safety change.

3. A compound subject is two or more subjects that go with the same verb. Underline the compound subject in each sentence.

    The king of France and two brothers made it happen.

    A major in the army and a physics professor went up.

    Ed Yost and Raven Industries began to design hot air balloons.

    Ed Yost and the Navy made important changes.

4. Irregular verbs do not add *-ed* to make the past tense. They change their form. Write the present tense of each bold verb.

    The king of France **thought** a man would die up in a balloon. _____

    So, two brothers **did** a test. _____

    Ed Yost and Raven Industries **began** to design hot air balloons. _____

    He **sold** hot air balloons for sports events. _____

Complete the following. The first one is done for you.

1. 20 As in all.

    ___4___ As in each group.

    How many groups?

    20 ÷ 4 = ___5___

    There are ___5___ groups.

    Check: ___4 x 5 = 20___

    ```
    AAAA
    AAAA
    AAAA
    AAAA
    AAAA
    ```

2. 20 As in all.

    _____ groups of As.

    How many in each group?

    20 ÷ 5 = _____

    There are _____ As in each group.

    Check: _____

3. 12 ☐ in all.

    3 ☐ in each group.

    How many groups?

    12 ÷ 3 = _____

    There are _____ groups.

    Check: _____

    ```
    ☐☐☐
    ☐☐☐
    ☐☐☐
    ☐☐☐
    ```

4. 12 ☐ in all.

    4 groups of ☐.

    How many in each group?

    12 ÷ 4 = _____

    There are _____ ☐ in each group.

    Check: _____

5. _____ Fs in all.

    _____ Fs in each group.

    How many groups?

    12 ÷ 2 = _____

    There are _____ groups.

    Check: _____

    ```
    FF
    FF
    FF
    FF
    FF
    FF
    ```

6. _____ Fs in all.

    _____ groups of Fs.

    How many in each group?

    12 ÷ 6 = _____

    There are _____ Fs in each group.

    Check: _____

FACTOID: It's almost impossible to tickle yourself. Try it!

Solve each problem.

1. Isabella wants to watch a show at 8:00 p.m. It is 7:23 p.m. How many more minutes is it until the show starts?

2. Cade's favorite show starts at 7:30 p.m. It is 90 minutes long. What time will the show end?

3. Taylor's favorite show started at 4:30 p.m. It is 30 minutes long. It is 4:53 p.m. right now. How many more minutes is the show on?

4. Melissa watched a movie that started at 7:00 p.m. It lasted 1 hour and 47 minutes. What time did the movie end?

5. Jonathan started watching a show at 4:16 p.m. He turned the television off at 5:37 p.m. How long did he watch television?

6. Chelsea watched 2 30-minute shows on Monday, 1 30-minute show on Wednesday, and 3 30-minute shows on Friday. How many hours of television did she watch that week?

CHARACTER CHECK: List five ways you can show caring to your friends and family members.

Write two exclamatory sentences and two declarative sentences. Use a word from the word bank in each sentence.

| attention | calmly | important | free | thousand |
| moment | snow | shiver | station | weird |

1. _____

2. _____

3. _____

4. _____

Where is the most exciting place you have ever been? Is it near where you live or far away? Describe this place. What makes it so exciting?

_____

_____

_____

_____

_____

_____

_____

Divide to solve each problem. Draw pictures to help you.

1.
$9 \div 3 = \underline{\textbf{3}}$

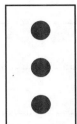

2.
$8 \div 2 = \underline{\hphantom{000}}$

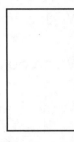

3.
$6 \div 2 = \underline{\hphantom{000}}$

4.
$16 \div 4 = \underline{\hphantom{000}}$

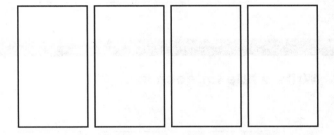

5.
$12 \div 6 = \underline{\hphantom{000}}$

6.
$18 \div 3 = \underline{\hphantom{000}}$

FITNESS FLASH: Stand with your feet together and stretch your arms straight up into the air without locking your elbows. How high can you reach?

173

Use the dictionary entry to answer the questions.

> **gem** \'jem\ *n* **1.** jewel **2.** A beloved or prized person or possession

1. What part of speech is *gem*? _____

2. Which definition of *gem* deals with precious stones? _____

3. Would *gemstone* come before or after *gem* in the dictionary? _____

4. Use *gem* in a sentence. _____

    _____

Write a title for each list.

5. _____
    sparrow
    wren
    blue jay
    parrot

6. _____
    paper
    paste
    scissors
    markers

7. _____
    lion
    rhino
    bear
    hippo

8. _____
    milk
    coffee
    water
    soda

9. _____
    eggs
    toast
    bagels
    bacon

10. _____
    fly
    bee
    wasp
    ant

Use a ruler to measure each object in centimeters. Then, measure again to the nearest inch.

1.  _____ centimeters   about _____ inches

2.  _____ centimeters   about _____ inch

3.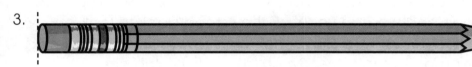

   _____ centimeters   about _____ inches

4.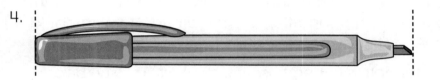

   _____ centimeters   about _____ inches

5.

   _____ centimeters   about _____ inches

6.

   _____ centimeters   about _____ inches

7. What do you notice about the measurements in centimeters compared to those in inches? _____

8. What explains this? _____

The Snow Child

Read the story.

Many years ago, there lived a woman and a man. As they grew older, they also grew sadder, for they had no children. One winter morning, the man looked out the window at the falling snow. "Let's build a snow child," he suggested to his wife. "Yes," said the woman, "a snow child just for us."

The man and the woman went outside and began to make a little girl out of snow. They made her legs, her arms, and her head. They used bits of sparkling blue ice for her eyes. When the man and woman finished, they stood back to look at what they had created. They could hardly believe their eyes. They had created a beautiful snow child. The woman kissed the snow child gently on the cheek. Suddenly, the snow child began to smile. She stretched out her arms. She stretched out her legs. She spun around and gave a little laugh. "I'm alive," she giggled with delight. Then, she ran and gave the old man and the woman a hug. Nothing could have made the couple happier. At last, they had the child they had longed for.

The days passed. Soon, the winter storms turned to spring showers. The sun began to warm the earth. The signs of spring were everywhere. But, as the days became warmer, the snow child became more and more unhappy. She would not go outside. "Come, little daughter. Why do you look so sad? Go outside and play with the other children," said the woman. The snow child did as she was told.

But before the snow child could join the other children, she disappeared. There was only a white mist where the girl had stood. The mist formed into a thin cloud and rose higher and higher, until it joined the clouds in the sky. The man and the woman wept bitterly at the loss of their dear little snow child. Once again, they were sad and lonely.

After many months, the days became shorter and the nights longer. The air was crisp and cool once again. Winter was coming. One night, as the first snow began to fall, the couple sat by the window remembering their dear little snow child. Suddenly, they heard a happy laugh and a familiar voice singing,

Winter is here. I am back with the snow. Do not fear, when comes spring I go. I will return with the snow each year, for you, my parents, are oh, so dear.

The couple ran to the door. They hugged their little snow child. How happy they were to be together again! The snow child stayed with them through each winter. Then, when spring came, she disappeared until winter returned to the couple's cottage again.

Use the story to answer the questions.

1. Why were the man and the woman sad at the beginning of the story?
   A. because they were growing old
   B. because they had no children
   C. because the winter was too cold

2. What brought the snow child to life?
   A. a fairy godmother
   B. a snowflake
   C. the woman's kiss

3. The ending *-er* often means "more." Sometimes, it is used to compare two things. The ending *-est* means "most." It is used to compare more than two things. Write a comparative word to complete each sentence.

   The days are getting _____ now that summer is here.

   That clown looks_____ than the one with the frown on his face.

   Jessie's hair is _____ than Claudia's.

   Ilene is three years _____ than Kevin.

   That statue is _____ on the shelf than I thought.

4. Write the base word for each word.

   warmer _____   shorter _____

   happier _____   older _____

5. Why would the snow child disappear in the spring?

   _____

   _____

6. In the story, what are some signs of spring?

   _____

   _____

7. In the story, what are some signs of winter?

   _____

   _____

Divide to solve each problem.

1. Kyle's fish store has 21 goldfish. The fish are in 3 aquariums. The same number of goldfish are in each aquarium. How many goldfish are in each aquarium?

   There are _____ goldfish.

   There are _____ aquariums.

   There are _____ goldfish in each aquarium.

2. Tia has 18 shoes in her closet. A pair of shoes is a group of 2 shoes. How many pairs of shoes does Tia have?

   Tia has _____ shoes.

   A pair is a group of _____ shoes.

   Tia has _____ pairs of shoes.

3. The egg carton has 12 eggs in it. There are 2 rows in the carton. How many eggs are in each row?

   The egg carton has _____ eggs.

   There are _____ rows in the carton.

   There are _____ eggs in each row.

4. Fiona has 16 sticks of gum. If she gives each of her 4 friends the same number of sticks of gum, how many sticks of gum will each of Fiona's friends have?

   Each of Fiona's friends will have _____ sticks of gum.

5. Ben earned 36 dollars for mowing 3 lawns on Saturday. Ben earned the same amount of money for each lawn. How much did he earn for each lawn?

   Ben earned _____ dollars for each lawn he mowed.

Find the area of each shape.

1.

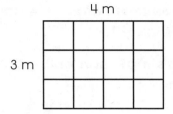

A = _____ sq. m

2.

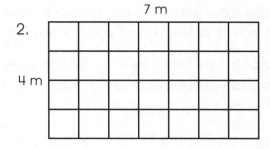

A = _____ sq. m

3.

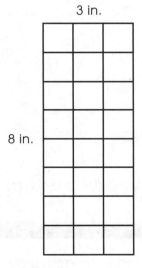

A = _____ sq. in.

4.

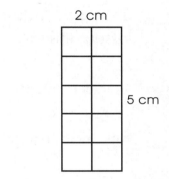

A = _____ sq. cm

5.

A = _____ sq. cm

6.

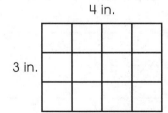

A = _____ sq. in.

A *simple sentence* has one subject and one verb. A *compound sentence* is two simple sentences joined with a conjunction like *and*. A *complex sentence* is a simple sentence combined with a group of words called a *dependent clause*. A dependent clause has a subject and a verb but is not a complete thought.

Read each sentence below. On the line, write *S* if it is a simple sentence, *C* if it is a compound sentence, and *CX* if it is a complex sentence.

1. _____ The goldfinch ate from the birdfeeder, and then it flew away.

2. _____ Brian went to the park on Sunday.

3. _____ Because Madeline has a beautiful voice, she's going to take singing lessons this fall.

4. _____ Felicia plays soccer every day.

5. _____ Although the temperature dropped last night, the plants were okay.

6. _____ Derek stopped at the library, but the book he ordered wasn't in yet.

Imagine that when you go to your mailbox one day, you find a treasure map with a letter addressed to you. Write a story about the letter and map. Who sent the letter? If you look for the treasure, do you find it? If you find it, what is it?

_____

_____

_____

_____

_____

_____

Divide to solve each problem.

1. Rusty wants to save 72 dollars. How many weeks will it take Rusty to save 72 dollars if he saves 9 dollars each week?

    Rusty wants to save _____ dollars.

    He saves _____ dollars each week.

    It will take Rusty _____ weeks to save 72 dollars.

2. Ms. Katz worked 40 hours this week. She worked 8 hours each day. How many days did she work this week?

    Ms. Katz worked _____ hours this week.

    She worked _____ hours each day.

    She worked _____ days this week.

3. There are 22 football players on the field. If there are 11 players on each team, how many teams are on the field?

    There are _____ football players on the field.

    There are _____ players on each team.

    There are _____ teams on the field.

4. Mrs. Edwards ordered 66 chairs and 11 tables for a banquet. Each table will have the same number of chairs. How many chairs will be at each table?

    There will be _____ chairs at each table.

The Ants Go Marching

Read the story.

Out of the blue, Aunt Cathy started laughing and hiccuping. Then, she and Heather sang, "The ants go marching one by one, hurrah, hurrah. The ants go marching one by one, hurrah, hurrah. The ants go marching one by one. The little one stops to have some fun. Then, they all go marching down to the ground to get out of the rain. Boom, boom, boom, boom. Boom, boom, boom, boom."

"Please stop," Chloe whined. She didn't want to hear all 50 verses of that song ever again. But, that didn't matter. They sang and sang, adding more and more verses while it continued to rain. Heather's dad was coming to jump-start the car. It was going to take him at least an hour, but it would feel even longer if Heather and Aunt Cathy didn't stop singing. Chloe kept chiming in, "Put a sock in it!" But, they pretended not to notice.

While they waited for Heather's dad, things started to get really exciting. Lightning crashed across the sky. Trees lit up, and birds screeched. With Aunt Cathy hiccuping and singing with Heather about ants, Chloe began to get, well, antsy. She said that they couldn't just lollygag all night. The sounds of thunder and the flashes of lightning were coming closer together.

Suddenly, lightning struck a tree by the river. Aunt Cathy got the hiccups scared right out of her. Heather stopped singing. Luckily, the downpour put out the fire from the lightning. After that, they kept their eyes peeled.

Then, headlights came at them head-on. They nearly jumped out of their skins. It couldn't be Heather's father. Chloe had just called him on her cell phone....

The Ants Go Marching

The ants go marching one by one, hurrah, hurrah!

The ants go marching one by one, hurrah, hurrah!

The ants go marching one by one.

The little one stops to have some fun.

Then, they all go marching down to the ground to get out of the rain.

Boom, boom, boom, boom!

Boom, boom, boom, boom!

Use the story to answer the questions.

1. An idiom is a phrase that means something different from the words that make it up. List three idioms you find in the story on page 182.

    _____

    _____

    _____

2. Write the matching word from the story for each meaning in the word bank.

antsy	**little**
skin	**lollygag**

    small   anxious

    _____   _____

    the outer covering on a body   to loaf or do nothing

    _____   _____

3. Write your own verse for the song "The Ants Go Marching." To keep the rhythm of the song, follow the pattern of the words in the verse on page 182.

    _____   _____

    _____   _____

    _____   _____

4. Predict what might happen next in the story. Write your own ending to the chapter.

    _____   _____

    _____   _____

    _____   _____

The Game of Summer, Step 2

Now that you have decided what your game will be about, here are some questions to answer before designing it.

1. What is the goal of your game? Will the players try to capture territory, collect objects, get to the finish line first, or something else?

    _____

    _____

2. What will you use for game pieces?

    _____

3. How will players know where to go on the board? Will they roll a die? Draw a card?

    _____

4. How many players can play your game?

    _____

5. What are the most important rules of your game?

    _____

    _____

    _____

6. What will your game board look like? Use the space on the next page to draw it.

Design Your Game Board

Here is a space to draw your game board. Look at the next page for an example of a simple game board.

Game Board Example

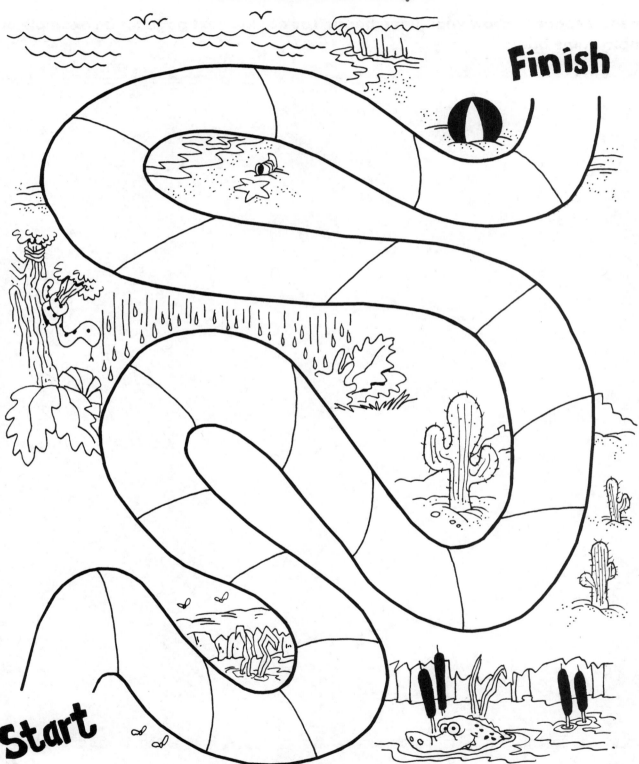

Finish

Start

My Body Homework

To keep your body working and looking its best, you should start good habits now and maintain them as you grow older. Use this checklist to keep yourself on track for the next week. Keep it on your bathroom mirror or next to your bed where it will remind you to do your "homework!"

	Sun.	Mon.	Tues.	Wed.	Thurs.	Fri.	Sat.
I slept at least 8 hours.							
I ate a healthful breakfast.							
I brushed my teeth this morning.							
I ate a healthful lunch.							
I washed my hands after using the bathroom.							
I exercised at least 30 minutes today.							
I drank at least 6 glasses of water.							
I stood and sat up straight.							
I ate a healthful dinner.							
I bathed.							
I brushed my teeth this evening.							

How Does Your Garden Grow?

Experience planting, caring for, harvesting and packaging vegetables by planting a small garden of radishes.

What you'll need:
paper cups
radish seeds
potting soil

What to do:

1. Fill the paper cups three-fourths full with soil.

2. Plant radish seeds according to the package directions. (Radishes are great for this activity as they are fast-growing vegetables, and you will be able to harvest them within 20 to 30 days.)

3. When they are ready to harvest, or pull, wash them and package them in sandwich bags. Enjoy!

Take It Outside!

Take a watch or timer outside and find an anthill. Look at the ants go in and out of the anthill for ten minutes. Count how many ants you see going in and out. What do they do if you put a few cookie crumbs near their home? What if you make a trail of crumbs? How many ants follow the trail?

With an adult, go outside and look at the stars. Ancient Greeks imagined lines between the stars that made pictures. Can you imagine a star picture? Draw the picture on a piece of paper in the dark. Did it turn out like you imagined?

Go on a pretend safari. Hide some plastic toy animals in your backyard. Make a list of where they are so you do not lose any. Lead a few friends or younger siblings through your yard to look for the animals. Be a safari guide and describe each animal you come upon in "the Wild." Include any fun facts you know about the animals.

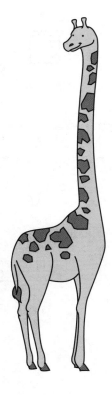

Fill in the missing numerals to show equivalent fractions.

1. $\dfrac{1}{3} = \dfrac{\square}{6} = \dfrac{\square}{9} = \dfrac{4}{\square} = \dfrac{5}{\square}$

2. $\dfrac{1}{4} = \dfrac{\square}{8} = \dfrac{\square}{12} = \dfrac{4}{\square} = \dfrac{\square}{20}$

3. $\dfrac{2}{3} = \dfrac{\square}{6} = \dfrac{6}{\square} = \dfrac{\square}{12} = \dfrac{10}{\square}$

4. $\dfrac{3}{4} = \dfrac{6}{\square} = \dfrac{9}{\square} = \dfrac{\square}{\square} = \dfrac{\square}{\square}$

5. $\dfrac{4}{5} = \dfrac{\square}{10}$

6. $\dfrac{3}{7} = \dfrac{\square}{21}$

7. $\dfrac{4}{7} = \dfrac{16}{\square}$

8. $\dfrac{3}{4} = \dfrac{21}{\square}$

9. $\dfrac{7}{8} = \dfrac{14}{\square}$

10. $\dfrac{5}{6} = \dfrac{\square}{18}$

11. $\dfrac{2}{7} = \dfrac{12}{\square}$

12. $\dfrac{2}{5} = \dfrac{\square}{20}$

Underline the pronoun that completes each sentence.

1. Dorian borrowed five books from the library, but he has lost one of (it, them).

2. At the fair, several kids lost (them, their) balloons.

3. Uri has two snakes as pets and loves (their, them) very much.

4. Javier remembered to floss (their, his) teeth before bed.

5. The hurricane made landfall at 3:00, and (it, them) is headed this way!

6. Each of the boys gets a sandwich for (her, his) lunch.

Capitalize the first, last, and all important words in a story or book title. Write each story title correctly.
EXAMPLE:

an exciting summer vacation _____**An Exciting Summer Vacation**_____

7. my ride on a horse _____

8. the day I missed school _____

9. fun, fabulous pets _____

10. a tornado drill _____

11. my summer project _____

FACTOID: Oceans cover more than 70 percent of Earth's surface.

Divide to solve the problems.

1. $4\overline{)24}$ 2. $4\overline{)16}$ 3. $7\overline{)21}$ 4. $9\overline{)81}$ 5. $6\overline{)18}$

6. $6\overline{)54}$ 7. $9\overline{)27}$ 8. $5\overline{)55}$ 9. $6\overline{)42}$ 10. $5\overline{)5}$

11. $3\overline{)24}$ 12. $4\overline{)28}$ 13. $9\overline{)36}$ 14. $2\overline{)14}$ 15. $1\overline{)9}$

16. $3\overline{)6}$ 17. $9\overline{)18}$ 18. $7\overline{)35}$ 19. $5\overline{)15}$ 20. $3\overline{)9}$

21. $7\overline{)42}$ 22. $9\overline{)45}$ 23. $4\overline{)4}$ 24. $7\overline{)63}$ 25. $2\overline{)6}$

26. $5\overline{)20}$ 27. $2\overline{)18}$ 28. $4\overline{)36}$ 29. $4\overline{)24}$ 30. $8\overline{)72}$

31. $6\overline{)6}$ 32. $8\overline{)64}$ 33. $6\overline{)36}$ 34. $5\overline{)45}$ 35. $3\overline{)18}$

Use the dictionary entries below to find the answers.

1.   Which definition best fits the word *cry* as it is used in this sentence?

     The little girl cried out for her mother.

     Definition number _____

2.   List other forms of the word *cute*. _____   _____

3.   Which part of speech is the word *cream*? _____

4.   Which definition best fits the word *crook* as it is used in this sentence?

     The crook stole the diamond from the museum.

     Definition number _____

5.   What is the definition of the word *dark*?

     _____

---

cream (noun)
  1. the yellowish white part of milk
crook (noun)
  1. a bent part; curve
I carry my umbrella in the crook of my arm.
  2. a shepherd's staff with a hook at
    the top
  3. a person who is not honest

cry (verb)
  1. to shed tears; weep.
The hungry baby cried.
  2. to call out loudly; shout.
The people in the burning building were crying for help.

cute (adjective)
  1. delightful or pretty.
This is the cutest puppy I have ever seen.

dark (adjective)
  1. having little or no light
The night was dark because the clouds covered the moon.

dash (verb)
  1. to move fast; rush
We dashed to the waiting bus.
  2. to destroy or ruin
Spraining my ankle dashed my hopes of running in the race.

Complete each sentence. Circle the measurement that makes the most sense.

1. My Dad is _____ tall.   6 inches   6 feet

2. My math book is _____ wide.   9 inches   9 feet

3. My big toe is _____ long.   I inch   I foot

4. My new baby sister is _____ long.   20 inches   20 feet

Measure the shape at the right with a ruler.

5. What is the length of the rectangle? _____ in.

6. What is the width of the rectangle? _____ in.

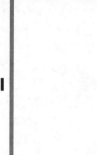

7. Add the measurements of the 4 sides of the rectangle
    to find its perimeter.

    ____ inches + ____ inches + ____ inches + ____ inches = _____ inches

194

Underline an adverb to complete each sentence.

1. Our puppy plays (more happily, happier) with children than with anyone else.

2. Jorge arrived (latest, most late) to class.

3. Please try to whisper (softer, more softly) while the baby sleeps.

4. Forrest jumped (most high, highest) of anyone in the competition.

5. The stars seem to shine (brightliest, most brightly) far from the city.

6. My brother completed the activity (carefullier, more carefully) than I did.

Similar words can have different shades of meaning. Write each word in the sentence where it makes the most sense.

7. **happy, overjoyed**

    Shannon was _____ to see her grandparents for the first time in nearly ten years.

    Paul was _____ that he could sleep in on Saturday morning.

8. **upset, outraged**

    Pedro felt _____ when he couldn't find his soccer cleats.

    Mrs. Kwan was _____ that the babysitter forgot to pick up the kids at school.

9. **gigantic, large**

    A _____ moth fluttered around the porch light.

    During the tsunami, several _____ waves nearly destroyed the village.

Find the area of each shape.

1.   7 yd.

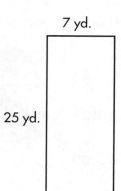

25 yd.

_____ sq. yd.

2.   6 in.

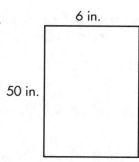

50 in.

_____ sq. in.

3.

        10 ft.

4 ft.

_____ sq. ft.

4.

        15 in.

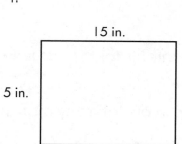

5 in.

_____ sq. in.

5.   4 yd.

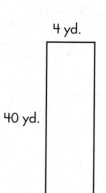

40 yd.

_____ sq. yd.

6.   8 yd.

20 yd.

_____ sq. yd.

FACTOID: Female great white sharks are usually larger than males.

Your teacher asks you to write a report about animals. In the report, you must answer all of the questions listed below. It would take a very long time to read the entire book, so you decide to use the table of contents to help you. Write the chapter and page number where you would look to answer each question.

Table of Contents

	Chapter	Page
1. How long do lions live?		
2. How fast do sailfish swim?		
3. What do snakes eat?		
4. How long does it take for robin eggs to hatch?		
5. Do spiders bite?		
6. Where do poison dart frogs live?		
7. What do beavers eat?		
8. How long do turtles live?		

Use the missing factor to help you find the quotient.

1.
$$2 \times \boxed{} = 8$$
$$8 \div 2 = \boxed{}$$

2.
$$3 \times \boxed{} = 9$$
$$9 \div 3 = \boxed{}$$

3.
$$4 \times \boxed{} = 16$$
$$16 \div 4 = \boxed{}$$

4.
$$8 \times \boxed{} = 40$$
$$40 \div 8 = \boxed{}$$

5.
$$5 \times \boxed{} = 25$$
$$25 \div 5 = \boxed{}$$

6.
$$6 \times \boxed{} = 18$$
$$18 \div 6 = \boxed{}$$

7.
$$4 \times \boxed{} = 12$$
$$12 \div 4 = \boxed{}$$

8.
$$7 \times \boxed{} = 42$$
$$42 \div 7 = \boxed{}$$

9.
$$3 \times \boxed{} = 15$$
$$15 \div 3 = \boxed{}$$

10.
$$9 \times \boxed{} = 81$$
$$81 \div 9 = \boxed{}$$

11.
$$2 \times \boxed{} = 10$$
$$10 \div 2 = \boxed{}$$

12.
$$2 \times \boxed{} = 4$$
$$4 \div 2 = \boxed{}$$

13.
$$5 \times \boxed{} = 20$$
$$20 \div 5 = \boxed{}$$

14.
$$3 \times \boxed{} = 6$$
$$6 \div 3 = \boxed{}$$

15.
$$6 \times \boxed{} = 36$$
$$36 \div 6 = \boxed{}$$

CHARACTER CHECK: Has anyone ever asked you to keep a secret for him or her? Were you able to do it? Are there any secrets that shouldn't be kept?

Unscramble and rewrite each sentence correctly. Add capital letters where they are needed. Write a period (.) or question mark (?) at the end of each sentence.

1. spiders do live where _____

2. very my hard studies brother _____

3. swim can like fish a he _____

4. blue the sky why is _____

5. water fish in live _____

6. store the go can when we to _____

7. the did go she to library why _____

8. is what name his _____

Have you ever written a letter on paper and sent it? Pick a friend, family member or famous person to write a letter to. What would you put in the letter?

_____

_____

_____

_____

_____

_____

_____

_____

Measure each object. Tell how much longer one object is than the other.

1.

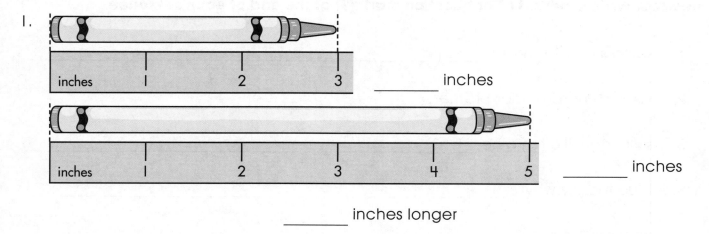

_____ inches

_____ inches

_____ inches longer

2.

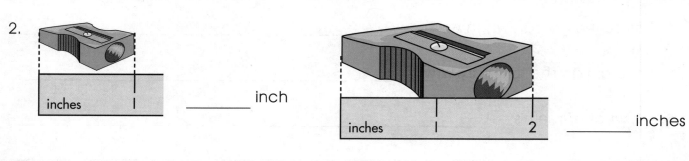

_____ inch

_____ inches

_____ inch longer

3.

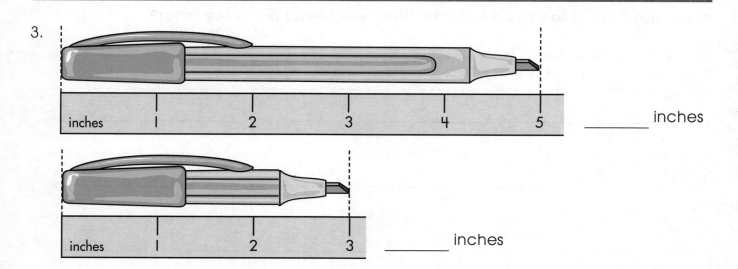

_____ inches

_____ inches

_____ inches longer

Draw one line of symmetry for each object.

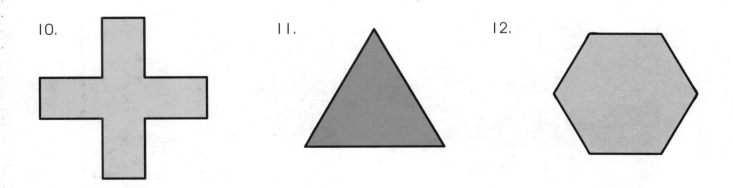

1.

2.

3.

4.

5.

6.

7.

8.

9.

Draw two lines of symmetry for each figure.

10.

11.

12.

BONUS

Natural Wonders

Earth's physical features are its natural formations. Match each formation with its definition by writing the correct number in each blank.

_____	river	1.	land rising high above the land around it
_____	bay	2.	land surrounded completely by water
_____	island	3.	piece of land surrounded by water on all but one side
_____	gulf	4.	inlet of a large water body that extends into the land; smaller than a gulf
_____	mountain	5.	Earth opening that spills lava, rock, and gases
_____	plain	6.	large inland body of water
_____	lake	7.	lowland between hills or mountains
_____	peninsula	8.	long, narrow body of water
_____	valley	9.	large area of flat grasslands
_____	volcano	10.	vast body of salt water
_____	ocean	11.	large area of a sea or ocean partially enclosed by land

Directions: Now, write each feature's number on the map.

Features Map

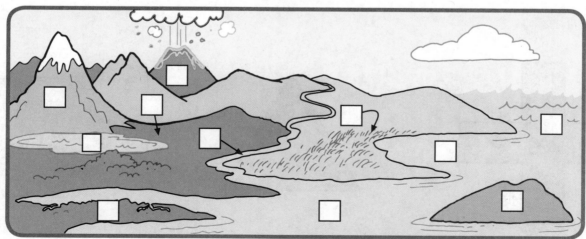

How Wet Is Wet?

Make several gauges and place them in different areas outside. Use the chart below to compare how much it has rained in different areas. Compare the amount of precipitation with that of the U.S. Weather Bureau (found in the newspaper or on the news).

What you'll need:
clear plastic glasses, a ruler with sixteenths, clear tape, an index card, masking tape, a pen

What to do:
To make a rain gauge, place the ruler so that it is just at the "floor" of your glass. (You want to measure the water that falls into the glass and not include its base.) Tape the ruler in place. Put your rain gauge in a flat, open area. After a rainfall, record the amount of water in the glass.

SNOW: You can use a ruler and a coffee can to measure snowfall. Put the coffee can in an open area. After snowfall, measure the inches of snow in the can using a ruler. Bring the can of snow inside. Let it melt. Pour it into a rain gauge. Write your observation on an index card.

Precipitation					
Name					
Address					
Date	Amount	Official	Date	Amount	Official

Use the index to find the correct answers, and then circle them.

Index	
Horses	55, 57–59
Houses	
Cave	34, 41–50
Modern	14, 18, 21
American Indian	67
Humans	
Adults	115–121, 127
Babies	89, 94–108
Children	109–114
Hunting	51, 56
Hurricanes	12, 17

1. Which of these pages will not help you learn about babies?

   A. page 89　　　　B. page 92　　　　C. page 97

2. Which page will help you learn about hunting?

   A. page 12　　　　B. page 56　　　　C. page 115

3. Which type of house is not found in the book?

   A. cave　　　　B. modern　　　　C. shingle

4. Which of these pages will not help you learn about houses?

   A. page 76　　　　B. page 45　　　　C. page 18

5. What will you learn about on page 111?

   A. adults　　　　B. children　　　　C. babies

6. Which page will help you learn about hurricanes?

   A. page 12　　　　B. page 67　　　　C. page 43

Circle each correct answer.

1. A wading pool holds about: 500 grams   500 liters   5,000 liters

2. A refrigerator weighs about: 90 grams   90 kilograms   9 kilograms

3. A nail weighs about: 1 gram   100 grams   1,000 grams

4. A small dog weighs about: 15 grams   50 grams   5,000 grams

Solve using addition and subtraction.

5. Warren brought 4 quarts of milk for the party. Ian brought 6 quarts of milk for the party. How many more quarts of milk did Ian bring than Warren?

   Ian brought _____ more quarts of milk than Warren.

6. Delaina's bag of fruit weighs 32 ounces. Ken's bag of fruit weighs 14 ounces. How many ounces do Delaina and Ken's bags weigh altogether?

   Delaina and Ken's bags of fruit weigh _____ ounces altogether.

7. Roberto had 18 gallons of paint to paint his entire house. He only used 11 gallons. How many gallons of paint does Roberto have left?

   Roberto has _____ gallons of paint left.

8. Jenna weighed 3 kilograms when she was born. Now she weighs 13 kilograms. How much weight did Jenna gain since she was born?

   Jenna gained _____ kilograms since she was born.

Add commas and quotation marks where they are needed. Use this symbol to add a comma ˄ and this symbol to add quotation marks ˅.

1. I asked, "Did you know that Renee lives in Billings, Montana?

2. "Mr. Chu is my neighbor said Grandpa.

3. Is Geneva's birthday in May?" asked Isabel.

4. "My mother and I shop at Miller's Market" I added.

5. What is your favorite day of the week? asked Wendy.

Add a simple sentence after each conjunction below to form a compound sentence.
EXAMPLE: Mr. Edwards is a teacher, but
               Mr. Edwards is a teacher, but I'm not in his class.

6. Dad is teaching Sean how to fix the car, but

_____

7. Hayley feeds the dog each morning, or

_____

8. It is supposed to rain on Saturday, so

_____

9. Chrissie just joined the basketball team, and

_____

Write two multiplication and two division equations for each fact family.

1.

_____ X _____ = _____

_____ X _____ = _____

_____ ÷ _____ = _____

_____ ÷ _____ = _____

2.

_____ X _____ = _____

_____ X _____ = _____

_____ ÷ _____ = _____

_____ ÷ _____ = _____

3.

_____ X _____ = _____

_____ X _____ = _____

_____ ÷ _____ = _____

_____ ÷ _____ = _____

4.

7
8 56

_____ X _____ = _____

_____ X _____ = _____

_____ ÷ _____ = _____

_____ ÷ _____ = _____

FITNESS FLASH: What is your favorite outdoor sport or game? Find a friend or family member who doesn't know how to play it and teach them how.

Divide each shape into the given amount of equal parts. Then, label each piece with the appropriate fraction.

1. thirds

2. halves

3. halves

4. thirds

5. fourths

6. fourths

7. halves

8. fifths

9. halves

10. fifths

Write the name of the person who is talking in each sentence.

1. Seth said, "Scott, you need to get out of bed." _____

2. "Is this your video game, Lamonte?" asked Khalil. _____

3. Lamonte replied, "No, Khalil, it is not my video game." _____

4. "Will you take the dog for a walk, Mona?" asked Mrs. Benson. _____

5. "Would you please go to the store for me?" Shazia asked. _____

Rewrite each sentence correctly. Add capital letters, periods, and question marks where they are needed.

6. bridget has a cat named spot

   _____

7. do robins eat worms

   _____

8. can i play with your soccer ball

   _____

9. my name is neyla

   _____

Divide or multiply to solve the problems.

1. $3\overline{)6}$
2. $8\overline{)16}$
3. $4\overline{)36}$
4. $6\overline{)54}$
5. $2\overline{)26}$

6. $8\overline{)40}$
7. $3\overline{)18}$
8. $2\overline{)6}$
9. $3\overline{)9}$
10. $2\overline{)16}$

11. $5\overline{)40}$
12. $9\overline{)27}$
13. $2\overline{)8}$
14. $1\overline{)7}$
15. $5\overline{)5}$

16. $7\overline{)42}$
17. $9\overline{)18}$
18. $9\overline{)81}$
19. $4\overline{)4}$
20. $7\overline{)28}$

21. $\begin{array}{r} 40 \\ \times\ 3 \\ \hline \end{array}$
22. $\begin{array}{r} 30 \\ \times\ 2 \\ \hline \end{array}$
23. $\begin{array}{r} 40 \\ \times\ 8 \\ \hline \end{array}$
24. $\begin{array}{r} 50 \\ \times\ 2 \\ \hline \end{array}$
25. $\begin{array}{r} 10 \\ \times\ 5 \\ \hline \end{array}$

26. $\begin{array}{r} 7 \\ \times\ 6 \\ \hline \end{array}$
27. $\begin{array}{r} 50 \\ \times\ 6 \\ \hline \end{array}$
28. $\begin{array}{r} 80 \\ \times\ 5 \\ \hline \end{array}$
29. $\begin{array}{r} 30 \\ \times\ 3 \\ \hline \end{array}$
30. $\begin{array}{r} 60 \\ \times\ 3 \\ \hline \end{array}$

31. $\begin{array}{r} 13 \\ \times\ 5 \\ \hline \end{array}$
32. $\begin{array}{r} 11 \\ \times\ 6 \\ \hline \end{array}$
33. $\begin{array}{r} 60 \\ \times\ 7 \\ \hline \end{array}$
34. $\begin{array}{r} 60 \\ \times\ 8 \\ \hline \end{array}$
35. $\begin{array}{r} 90 \\ \times\ 2 \\ \hline \end{array}$

An *analogy* compares two pairs of items based on a similar relationship between the items. Write the correct word from the word bank to complete each analogy.

dog	ground	window	~~water~~	trees	cow

EXAMPLE:

Car is to road as ship is to _____ **water** _____ .

1. Bird is to sky as worm is to _____ .

2. City is to buildings as forest is to _____ .

3. Knob is to door as pane is to _____ .

4. Foal is to horse as calf is to _____ .

5. Quack is to duck as woof is to _____ .

Write three sentences. Use a word from the word bank in each sentence. Use capital letters, periods, question marks, and exclamation points where they are needed.

adult	after	ready	bored
job	prepare	spring	work

6. _____

7. _____

8. _____

Answer the questions based on the number lines.

1. Are the fractions $\frac{1}{6}$ and $\frac{2}{3}$ equivalent? _____

    Name 2 other fractions that are equivalent. _____ _____

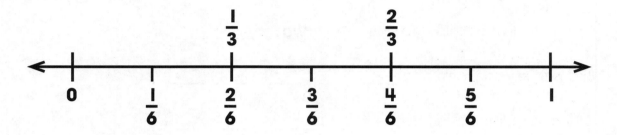

2. Are the fractions $\frac{1}{8}$ and $\frac{1}{4}$ equivalent? _____

    Name 2 other fractions that are equivalent. _____ _____

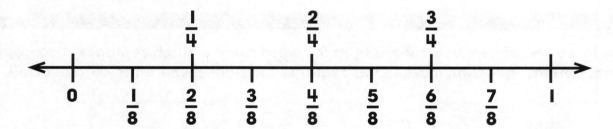

3. Write 2 fractions that are equivalent to $\frac{1}{5}$.

    $\frac{1}{5}$ = _____ = _____

FACTOID: Houseflies can taste with their feet.

Guide to Summer Fun, Final Step

Now you are ready to gather all your adventures together into a guidebook! Each page will provide details about one summer activity, including tips for making the most of the experience. For ideas on how your book could look, look at the examples on the next page.

What you'll need:
- details about each activity from Step 2 on p. 162
- sheets of paper (one for each activity)
- markers, colored pencils, or crayons
- stapler
- glue or tape

What you'll do:
1. Plan to use at least one side of a sheet of paper for each activity. You can use both sides, too. Write the name of the activity at the top of each page.

2. Write and illustrate each activity page. Make sure to include the most important and fun details about each activity. Remember, you're making a guide for someone else to follow. Include instructions, too. You can draw the pictures yourself or print out photos and glue or tape them to the page.

3. Make a front cover for your guidebook. The front cover should include the title of your book and the name of the author—you! Include a picture of your favorite summer activity, too.

4. Put your pages in order. You can organize them by type of activity, by when you did the activity, in alphabetical order, or in any way that makes sense to you.

5. Staple your book pages and cover together. If you need help, ask an adult.

6. Share your guidebook with your family and friends!

Finished Product Example

Here is one way you could put together a page for your guidebook:

Water Balloon Fight

Water balloons are exciting and refreshing on a hot summer day. Here are five tips for how to have a fun water balloon fight.

1. Buy some water balloons.
2. Get your friends together.
3. Fill your balloons with water. Make sure there are plenty for everyone.
4. Put the balloons in buckets all around the yard.
5. Throw the balloons at each other!

Here are five good water balloon safety rules to follow.

1. Don't hit anyone in the face with a water balloon.
2. Don't gang up on anyone.
3. Don't throw water balloons at people who aren't part of the game.
4. Be careful around smaller kids who might be playing.
5. Be a good sport!

The Game of Summer, Final Step

Now it's time to make your board game!

What you'll need:
- markers, colored pencils, or crayons
- construction paper
- poster board (for cards)
- cardboard
- scissors
- glue
- dice
- an old board game (you could re-use the board and tokens for your own game)

What you'll do:
1. Play a practice game with your game board drawing. Use pieces of paper for game pieces. Playing a practice game will help you figure out the details of your game before you invite friends and family to play it.

2. Write down the final version of the rules.

3. Make the final version of your game board.

4. Make the pieces for your game.

5. Invite your family and friends to play. Have fun!

Near My State

Use a map of the United States to locate your state. Write the names of the bordering states/countries and/or bodies of water on the chart below. Write each one in its correct location relative to your state.

Northwest	North	Northeast
West	My State	East
	Draw an outline of your state.	
Southwest	South	Southeast

Cool Color

Does color have anything to do with temperature?

You you'll need:
- 2 identical glasses
- one 9" x 12" sheet of black paper
- one 9" x 12" sheet of white paper
- masking tape
- an index card
- a pencil
- a pen
- an outside thermometer
- water
- scissors

Copy the Cool Color chart onto the index card.

Cool Color				
Name _____				

What to do:

Wrap one glass with black paper and one with white paper. Tape the paper closed. Cut off the excess paper. Fill each glass with the same amount of water. Set both glasses in a sunny spot. Leave them there for at least an hour. Then, put the thermometer into each glass and record the temperature of each on the Cool Color chart. Also, write on the chart what you concluded from this experiment. Do this experiment at least two more times to verify your conclusion. Try other colors to see if there is any difference.

Note: The water in the jar wrapped with black paper should be warmer because the black paper absorbs more heat than the white.

BONUS

Take It Outside!

Collect small outdoor objects like a pinecone, a leaf, a flower, and a nut. Look at each item. If you cut it in half, would the two sides look the same and have the same parts? If they would, then the object is symmetrical. How many symmetrical objects can you find?

On a hot day, place an outside thermometer in a sunny spot. Go and play for 10 minutes. Come back and write down the temperature. Then, put the thermometer in the shade for 10 minutes. Is it worth it to stay under a tree?

Ask an adult to help you figure out when the moon will be visible in the sky today. It could be during the day or after dark. Then, go outside with an adult and find the moon. List as many phrases as you can think of to describe where you see the moon, such as "over my house" and "next to the pine tree." Then, if it's not too late, wait an hour and check the moon's position again. Where is it now?

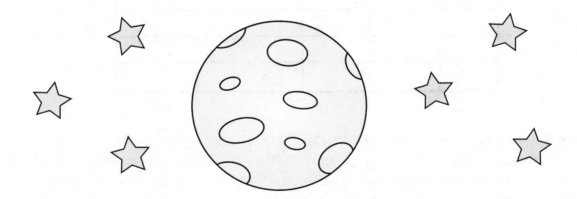

Answer Key

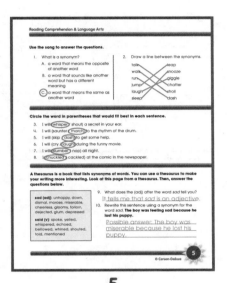

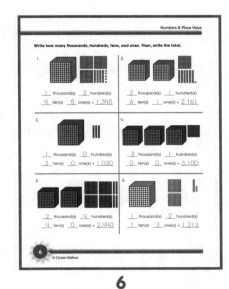

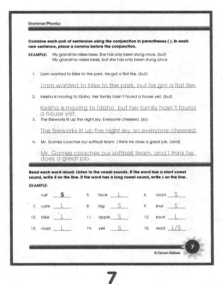

Page 5 — Reading Comprehension & Language Arts

Use the song to answer the questions.

1. What is a synonym?
   A. a word that means the opposite of another word
   B. a word that sounds like another word but has a different meaning
   (C.) a word that means the same as another word

2. Draw a line between the synonyms.
   talk — chatter
   walk — dash
   run — stroll
   jump — leap
   laugh — giggle
   sleep — snooze

Circle the word in parentheses that would fit best in each sentence.

3. I will (whisper/shout) a secret in your ear.
4. I will (saunter/march) to the rhythm of the drum.
5. I will (skip/dash) to get some help.
6. I will (cry/laugh) during the funny movie.
7. I will (slumber/nap) all night.
8. I (chuckled/cackled) at the comic in the newspaper.

A thesaurus is a book that lists synonyms of words. You can use a thesaurus to make your writing more interesting. Look at this page from a thesaurus. Then, answer the questions below.

sad (adj): unhappy, down, dismal, morose, miserable, cheerless, gloomy, forlorn, dejected, glum, depressed

said (v): spoke, yelled, whispered, echoed, bellowed, whined, shouted, told, mentioned

9. What does the (adj) after the word sad tell you?
   It tells me that sad is an adjective.

10. Rewrite this sentence using a synonym for the word sad. The boy was feeling sad because he lost his puppy.
    Possible answer: The boy was miserable because he lost his puppy.

Page 6 — Numbers & Place Value

Write how many thousands, hundreds, tens, and ones. Then, write the total.

1. __1__ thousand(s) __3__ hundred(s) __4__ ten(s) __5__ one(s) = 1,345
2. __2__ thousand(s) __1__ hundred(s) __6__ ten(s) __1__ one(s) = 2,161
3. __1__ thousand(s) __0__ hundred(s) __3__ ten(s) __0__ one(s) = 1,030
4. __3__ thousand(s) __1__ hundred(s) __0__ ten(s) __0__ one(s) = 3,100
5. __2__ thousand(s) __4__ hundred(s) __4__ ten(s) __0__ one(s) = 2,440
6. __1__ thousand(s) __2__ hundred(s) __1__ ten(s) __3__ one(s) = 1,213

Page 7 — Grammar/Phonics

Combine each pair of sentences using the conjunction in parentheses ( ). In each new sentence, place a comma before the conjunction.

EXAMPLE: My grandma raises bees. She has only been stung once. (but)
My grandma raises bees, but she has only been stung once.

1. Liam wanted to bike to the park. He got a flat tire. (but)
   Liam wanted to bike to the park, but he got a flat tire.

2. Keisha is moving to Idaho. Her family hasn't found a house yet. (but)
   Keisha is moving to Idaho, but her family hasn't found a house yet.

3. The fireworks lit up the night sky. Everyone cheered. (so)
   The fireworks lit up the night sky, so everyone cheered.

4. Mr. Gomez coaches our softball team. I think he does a great job. (and)
   Mr. Gomez coaches our softball team, and I think he does a great job.

Read each word aloud. Listen to the vowel sounds. If the word has a short vowel sound, write S on the line. If the word has a long vowel sound, write L on the line.

EXAMPLE:
rust __S__   5. face __L__   6. clock __S__
7. cute __L__   8. big __S__   9. shut __S__
10. bike __L__   11. apple __S__   12. boat __L__
13. road __L__   14. yell __S__   15. read __L/S__

Page 8 — Numbers & Place Value

Write each number in expanded form.

		Thousands	Hundreds	Tens	Ones
1.	9,516 =	9,000 +	500 +	10 +	6
2.	2,358 =	2,000 +	300 +	50 +	8
3.	1,407 =	1,000 +	400 +	0 +	7
4.	921 =	0 +	900 +	20 +	1
5.	7,800 =	7,000 +	800 +	0 +	0
6.	3,264 =	3,000 +	200 +	60 +	4
7.	5,182 =	5,000 +	100 +	80 +	2
8.	614 =	0 +	600 +	10 +	4
9.	4,073 =	4,000 +	0 +	70 +	3
10.	9,530 =	9,000 +	500 +	30 +	0

FITNESS FLASH: Stand up straight with a chair right behind you. Stretch your arms straight in front of you and slowly sit. Stop right before your bottom touches the chair and slowly stand up again. Repeat this 10 times.

Page 9 — Addition/Subtraction

Add to solve each problem.

1. 9 + 7 = 16
2. 2 + 3 = 5
3. 0 + 2 = 2
4. 8 + 3 = 11
5. 5 + 2 = 7
6. 4 + 4 = 8
7. 17 + 1 = 18
8. 4 + 8 = 12
9. 3 + 1 = 4
10. 2 + 7 = 9
11. 1 + 2 = 3
12. 6 + 2 = 8
13. 7 + 6 = 13
14. 5 + 9 = 14
15. 15 + 3 = 18

Subtract to solve each problem.

16. 4 − 2 = 2
17. 12 − 7 = 5
18. 6 − 4 = 2
19. 9 − 4 = 5
20. 13 − 5 = 8
21. 11 − 4 = 7
22. 19 − 6 = 13
23. 6 − 3 = 3
24. 3 − 3 = 0
25. 17 − 7 = 10
26. 17 − 8 = 9
27. 7 − 5 = 2
28. 3 − 0 = 3
29. 20 − 3 = 17
30. 12 − 4 = 8

FACTOID: Honeybees communicate with each other by dancing.

Page 11 — Reading Comprehension & Language Arts

Use the story to answer the questions.

1. Write T before the statements that are true and F before the statements that are false.
   __F__ The author is writing about his sister.
   __F__ Aunt Antonym is the real name of the author's aunt.
   __T__ Aunt Antonym thinks monkeys are ugly.
   __T__ Aunt Antonym wanted to sit in the back at the dolphin show because she didn't like to get wet.

2. Why did the author call his aunt Aunt Antonym?
   because she always says or does the opposite of the rest of the family

3. An antonym is a word that means the opposite of another word. For example, an antonym of big is little. Write a word from the story that is an antonym for each word below.
   north — south   ugly — adorable
   black — white   front — back
   dry — wet   hungry — full
   stay — go   brother — sister

4. Write the past tense for each verb.
   begin — began   think — thought
   say — said   ride — rode
   sit — sat   is — was
   have — had   wish — wished

Answer Key

You have discovered a hidden treasure! Round the value in each treasure chest to the nearest hundred. The first one is done for you.

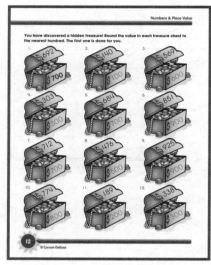

1. $5,692$ — **700**
2. $5,126$ — **100**
3. $5,569$ — **600**
4. $5,303$ — **300**
5. $5,684$ — **700**
6. $5,851$ — **900**
7. $5,712$ — **700**
8. $5,476$ — **500**
9. $5,925$ — **900**
10. $5,774$ — **800**
11. $5,189$ — **200**
12. $5,338$ — **300**

12

Count by 2. Write the missing numbers.

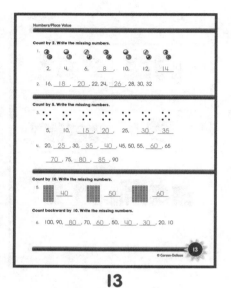

1. 2, 4, 6, _8_, 10, 12, _14_

2. 16, _18_, _20_, 22, 24, _26_, 28, 30, 32

Count by 5. Write the missing numbers.

3. 5, 10, _15_, _20_, 25, _30_, _35_

4. 20, _25_, 30, _35_, _40_, 45, 50, 55, _60_, 65, _70_, 75, _80_, _85_, 90

Count by 10. Write the missing numbers.

5. _40_   _50_   _60_

Count backward by 10. Write the missing numbers.

6. 100, 90, _80_, 70, _60_, 50, _40_, _30_, 20, 10

13

Read each word aloud. Then, write *short* or *long* for each vowel sound.

1. bug _short_ 　 2. cake _long_
3. jut _short_ 　 4. hum _short_
5. road _long_ 　 6. catch _short_
7. cube _long_ 　 8. lock _short_
9. sick _short_ 　 10. mild _long_
11. mop _short_ 　 12. these _long_
13. street _long_ 　 14. log _short_
15. spy _long_ 　 16. goat _long_

Words that name holidays, places, and products are proper nouns. Underline the proper noun or nouns in each sentence.

17. Have you ever been to <u>Portland</u>, <u>Oregon</u>?
18. Let's make cards for <u>Valentine's Day</u>.
19. My grandmother lives in <u>Japan</u>.
20. We always buy <u>Papa Louie's</u> pizza when we have family movie night.
21. Our neighbors moved here from <u>Chicago</u>, <u>Illinois</u>.
22. I'd like a glass of orange juice and a bowl of <u>Crunch Os</u> for breakfast.
23. Are you going to wear green on <u>St. Patrick's Day</u>?

14

Circle the numeral that is the least.

1. 173, (149), 156, 206, 347, 165
2. 699, 943, 943, 878, (566), 903
3. 510, (430), 530, 770, 680, 820
4. (390), 745, 845, 691, 759, 425
5. 941, 812, 852, 814, 916, (804)

Circle the numeral that is the greatest.

6. 746, (981), 873, 699, 870, 847
7. 633, (709), 599, 671, 433, 598
8. 695, 768, 845, (871), 555, 796
9. 493, 561, 664, 793, (990), 889
10. 567, 765, 675, 783, 623, (805)

Use greater than (>) and less than (<) signs to compare numerals.

11. 439 _<_ 670 　 944 _>_ 872 　 730 _<_ 750
12. 610 _>_ 603 　 567 _<_ 576 　 887 _<_ 891
13. 991 _>_ 919 　 499 _<_ 500 　 635 _>_ 471
14. 781 _<_ 902 　 1000 _>_ 998 　 549 _<_ 798
15. 473 _>_ 374 　 895 _<_ 958 　 768 _>_ 391
16. 399 _<_ 405 　 818 _<_ 881 　 914 _<_ 941

15

BONUS

Making a Compass

A compass is a magnet that can identify geographic direction. It is very easy and a lot of fun to make your own compass!

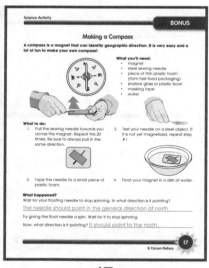

What you'll need:
- magnet
- steel sewing needle
- piece of thin plastic foam (from fast-food packaging)
- shallow glass or plastic bowl
- masking tape
- water

What to do:
1. Pull the sewing needle towards you across the magnet. Repeat this 20 times. Be sure to always pull in the same direction.
2. Test your needle on a steel object. If it is not yet magnetized, repeat step #1.
3. Tape the needle to a small piece of plastic foam.
4. Float your magnet in a dish of water.

What happened?
Wait for your floating needle to stop spinning. In what direction is it pointing?
The needle should point in the general direction of north.

Try giving the float needle a spin. Wait for it to stop spinning.

Now, what direction is it pointing? _It should point to the north._

17

BONUS

Leaning Into Summer

Why isn't it summer all year long? The seasons change because Earth is tilted like the Leaning Tower of Pisa. As Earth orbits the sun, it stays tilting in the same direction in space.

Let's look at the seasons in the Northern Hemisphere. When the North Pole is tilting toward the sun, the days become warmer and longer. It is summer. Six months later, the North Pole tilts away from the sun. The days become cooler and shorter. It is winter.

Directions: Label the Northern Hemisphere's seasons on the chart below. Write a make-believe weather forecast for each season. Each forecast should show what the weather is like in your region for that season.

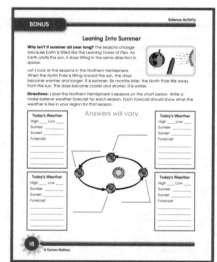

Answers will vary.

Today's Weather
High ____ Low ____
Sunrise ____
Sunset ____
Forecast ____

Today's Weather
High ____ Low ____
Sunrise ____
Sunset ____
Forecast ____

Today's Weather
High ____ Low ____
Sunrise ____
Sunset ____
Forecast ____

Today's Weather
High ____ Low ____
Sunrise ____
Sunset ____
Forecast ____

18

Answer Key

Page 19 — Phonics/Writing

Look at each word. Write how many vowels you see. Then, read each word aloud. Write how many vowel sounds you hear.

		Vowels	Vowel Sounds			Vowels	Vowel Sounds
1.	muzzle	2	2	9. radio		3	3
2.	cookies	4	2	10. merit		2	2
3.	socks	1	1	11. deep		2	1
4.	alphabet	3	3	12. wanted		2	2
5.	oak	2	1	13. heart		2	1
6.	junk	1	1	14. useful		2	2
7.	pilot	2	2	15. beautiful		5	3
8.	melting	2	2	16. otter		2	2

Think about your favorite food. Describe this food using each of your five senses. What do you see, hear, feel, smell, and taste?

Answers will vary.

Page 20 — Addition & Subtraction

Add or subtract to solve each problem.

1. There are 13 bananas. Kit takes 5. How many bananas are left? **8**
2. The Nowaks have 6 apples. Mrs. Nowak buys 5 more. How many apples do they have now? **11**
3. The store has 11 boxes of plums. 4 boxes of plums are sold. How many boxes are left? **7**
4. Together, Holly and her sister bought 18 bananas. Holly bought 8 bananas. How many bananas did her sister buy? **10** $8 + 10 = 18$
5. Mrs. Chang has 17 hats. 3 of the hats have bows. How many hats do not have bows? **14**

Page 21 — Measurement & Data

Yvette asked her classmates about their pets. She made this bar graph to show the results.

Our Pets

Use the bar graph to answer the questions.

1. Which pet do the most students have? **Cat**
2. How many students have a dog or a cat? **14**
3. How many students have pets? **21**
4. How many students did Yvette talk to? **25**
5. How many students have either a fish or a turtle? **7**

Page 22 — Language Arts

Write the homonym from the word bank that makes sense with the context clues in each pair of sentences.

tire   break   mean   straw   land   glasses   book   free

1. Be careful not to **break** Mom's favorite vase. Should we take a **break** from practice to eat lunch?
2. Mom will **book** an appointment for Monday. Have you read the new **book** by that author?
3. What do you **mean** by that? The dog that lives next door is **mean**, so let's stay away.
4. My cat is so old that chasing a mouse will **tire** her out. We got a flat **tire** when we drove to Florida.
5. The plane is due to **land** at 6:00 tonight. The large areas of **land** on Earth are called continents.
6. The zookeeper lifted the door to **free** the bird. I can't believe we read enough books to earn **free** pizza!
7. After you finish, set your lemonade **glasses** on the counter. I am going to get new **glasses** to help me see the board.
8. The farmer keeps **straw** in the barn during the winter. Can you hand me a **straw** for my milk shake?

Page 23 — Numbers

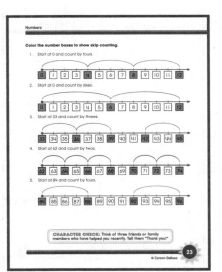

Color the number boxes to show skip counting.

1. Start at 0 and count by fours.
2. Start at 0 and count by sixes.
3. Start at 33 and count by threes.
4. Start at 62 and count by twos.
5. Start at 84 and count by fours.

CHARACTER CHECK: Think of three friends or family members who have helped you recently. Tell them "Thank you!"

Page 24 — Grammar

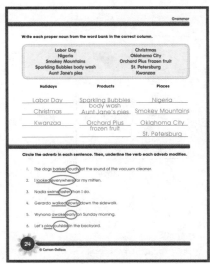

Write each proper noun from the word bank in the correct column.

Labor Day   Christmas   Nigeria   Oklahoma City   Smokey Mountains   Orchard Plus frozen fruit   Sparkling Bubbles body wash   St. Petersburg   Aunt Jane's pies   Kwanzaa

Holidays	Products	Places
Labor Day	Sparkling Bubbles body wash	Nigeria
Christmas	Aunt Jane's pies	Smokey Mountains
Kwanzaa	Orchard Plus frozen fruit	Oklahoma City
		St. Petersburg

Circle the adverb in each sentence. Then, underline the verb each adverb modifies.

1. The dogs barked loudly at the sound of the vacuum cleaner.
2. I looked everywhere for my mitten.
3. Nadia swims faster than I do.
4. Gerardo walked slowly down the sidewalk.
5. Wynona awoke early on Sunday morning.
6. Let's play outside in the backyard.

Answer Key

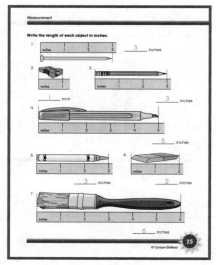
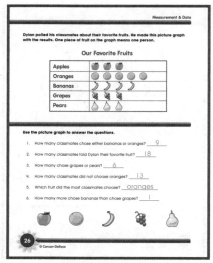
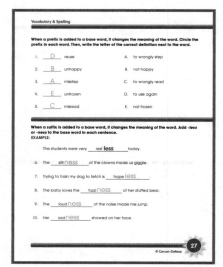

Measurement

Write the length of each object in inches.

1. 3 inches
2. 1 inch   3. 3 inches
4. 5 inches
5. 3 inches   6. 2 inches
7. 6 inches

25

Measurement & Data

Dylan polled his classmates about their favorite fruits. He made this picture graph with the results. One piece of fruit on the graph means one person.

Our Favorite Fruits

Apples	🍎🍎🍎
Oranges	🍊🍊🍊🍊🍊
Bananas	🍌🍌🍌🍌
Grapes	🍇🍇🍇
Pears	🍐🍐

Use the picture graph to answer the questions.

1. How many classmates chose either bananas or oranges? 9
2. How many classmates told Dylan their favorite fruit? 18
3. How many chose grapes or pears? 6
4. How many classmates did not choose oranges? 13
5. Which fruit did the most classmates choose? oranges
6. How many more chose bananas than chose grapes? 1

26

Vocabulary & Spelling

When a prefix is added to a base word, it changes the meaning of the word. Circle the prefix in each word. Then, write the letter of the correct definition next to the word.

1. D reuse   A. to wrongly step
2. B unhappy   B. not happy
3. A misstep   C. to wrongly read
4. E unfrozen   D. to use again
5. C misread   E. not frozen

When a suffix is added to a base word, it changes the meaning of the word. Add -less or -ness to the base word in each sentence.
EXAMPLE:
The students were very rest**less** today.

6. The silli**ness** of the clowns made us giggle.
7. Trying to train my dog to fetch is hope**less**.
8. The baby loves the fuzzi**ness** of her stuffed bear.
9. The loud**ness** of the noise made me jump.
10. Her sad**ness** showed on her face.

27

Time

Write the time two ways. The first one is done for you.

1. 7 o'clock / 7:00
2. 12 o'clock / 12:00
3. 11 o'clock / 11:00
4. 10 o'clock / 10:00
5. 6 o'clock / 6:00
6. 5 o'clock / 5:00
7. 9 o'clock / 9:00
8. 8 o'clock / 8:00
9. 2 o'clock / 2:00

31

Reading Comprehension/Grammar

Use the passage to answer the questions.

1. Circle the sentence that tells the main idea.
   A. Birds are unique animals.
   B. The adult bird teaches its babies how to fly and find food.
   C. Birds are one of the few animals that lay eggs.

2. Fill in the blanks with the correct answers.
   Birds are the only animals that have feathers.
   Birds do not have teeth.
   Birds lay eggs.
   Birds build nests to protect their eggs.

3. Number the sentences in the order that they happen.
   3 The adult birds bring food to the baby birds in the nest.
   2 The mother bird sits on the nest to keep the eggs warm.
   1 Birds build a nest to protect their eggs.
   4 The adult birds teach their babies how to fly and find food.

4. Write a T if the sentence is true. Write an F if the sentence is false.
   F All birds can fly.
   T Flying helps birds find food.
   T Flying protects birds from their enemies.
   F Birds migrate to stay away from their enemies.
   F Some birds have large teeth.

5. What does migrate mean?
   A. to hide under trees
   B. to fly to other places
   C. to find shelter

Action verbs tell what the subject of a sentence does. Circle the action verb in each sentence.
6. Birds fly with the help of their feathers.
7. Birds eat with their beaks instead of teeth.
8. Birds build nests for their eggs.
9. Baby birds hatch from eggs.
10. Adult birds bring their baby birds food.

33

Addition

Add to solve each problem.

1. 23 + 42 = 65
2. 64 + 25 = 89
3. 47 + 34 = 81
4. 13 + 45 = 58
5. 55 + 30 = 85

6. 70 + 29 = 99
7. 82 + 11 = 93
8. 74 + 23 = 97
9. 58 + 41 = 99
10. 26 + 33 = 59

11. 12 + 77 = 89
12. 83 + 13 = 96
13. 41 + 37 = 78
14. 19 + 60 = 79
15. 22 + 37 = 59

16. 15 + 72 = 87
17. 18 + 81 = 99
18. 84 + 12 = 96
19. 27 + 62 = 89
20. 46 + 41 = 87

21. 52 + 36 = 88
22. 75 + 10 = 85
23. 24 + 43 = 67
24. 51 + 27 = 78
25. 29 + 50 = 79

26. 31 + 55 = 86
27. 47 + 32 = 79
28. 19 + 30 = 49
29. 62 + 37 = 99
30. 33 + 52 = 85

34

Answer Key

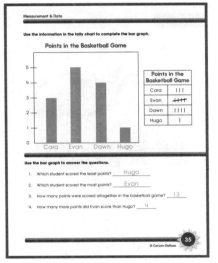
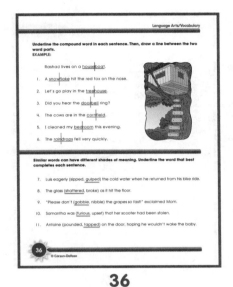
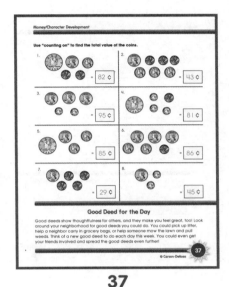

Answer Key

Read each sentence. Then, write the letter of the underlined word's definition.
EXAMPLE:

B The superhero can fly.   A. a small winged insect

A The frog ate the fly.   B. to move through the air

1. **A** Please turn on the light.   A. a lamp
   B The backpack is light.   B. not heavy

2. **B** Store the books in the box.   A. a place to buy things
   A I bought a shirt at the store.   B. to put away for the future

3. **B** Toss a coin in the well.   A. healthy
   A Are you feeling well?   B. a hole to access underground water

If you could keep only three of your toys and had to give the rest away, which three toys would you keep? Why?

Answers will vary.

41

Find the Landmarks

Geographers can tell us how places are the same and how they are different. Where you live is different from where your friend lives. Maybe you live southwest of school while your friend lives north of the school.

Directions: Write the names and draw pictures of landmarks that are found near your school. Place each one the chart in its correct location relative to your school.

Northwest	North	Northeast
West	School	East
Southwest	South	Southeast

Answers will vary.

43

The Life Cycle of a Frog

The frog goes through many changes during its life. Read about the frog's life cycle below. Then, complete the word puzzle using what you have learned.

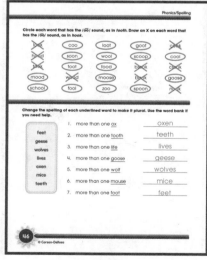

The adult frog eats insects and will lay a new mass of eggs.

The frog's life begins as a mass of eggs called spawn.

The young frog leaves the water. It begins breathing with lungs like a land animal.

Tadpoles hatch and feed on algae. They breathe with gills like fish.

The tadpole grows legs—first hind and then front.

Across:
1. Tadpoles feed on ___.
5. A mass of eggs is called ___.
6. Tadpoles breathe with ___.
8. The frog's changes are called its life.

Down:
2. Adult frogs breathe with ___.
3. Eggs hatch into ___.
4. Adult frogs eat ___.
7. Tadpoles grow ___.

44

Use the information in the tally chart to complete the picture graph.

Shapes Around the Kitchen

Triangles	▲▲▲▲▲▲
Stars	☆☆☆☆☆☆☆☆☆☆
Squares	■■■■■■■■
Circles	●●●●●

Shapes Around the Kitchen

▲	++++ I
☆	++++ ++++
■	++++ III
●	++++

Use the picture graph to answer the questions below.

1. What shape is seen the most around the kitchen?   star
2. How many more squares ■ are there than circles ●?   3
3. What shape is seen the least around the kitchen?   circle
4. How many more stars ☆ are there than triangles ▲?   4

45

Circle each word that has the /o͞o/ sound, as in tooth. Draw an X on each word that has the /o͝o/ sound, as in hook.

look (X), coo, loot, goof, cook (X)
hood (X), soon, wool, scoop, cool
took (X), toot, food, brook (X), chalk (X)
mood, wood (X), moose, book (X), goose
school, fool, zoo, spoon, nook (X)

Change the spelling of each underlined word to make it plural. Use the word bank if you need help.

Word bank: feet, geese, wolves, lives, oxen, mice, teeth

1. more than one ox   oxen
2. more than one tooth   teeth
3. more than one life   lives
4. more than one goose   geese
5. more than one wolf   wolves
6. more than one mouse   mice
7. more than one foot   feet

46

Subtract to solve each problem.

1. 86 − 32 = 54
2. 52 − 12 = 40
3. 67 − 45 = 22
4. 95 − 30 = 65
5. 87 − 26 = 61

6. 39 − 13 = 26
7. 66 − 46 = 20
8. 38 − 14 = 24
9. 75 − 52 = 23
10. 88 − 37 = 51

11. 47 − 15 = 32
12. 96 − 73 = 23
13. 58 − 54 = 4
14. 81 − 21 = 60
15. 57 − 33 = 24

16. 36 − 14 = 22
17. 87 − 77 = 10
18. 70 − 30 = 40
19. 65 − 50 = 15
20. 99 − 73 = 26

21. 97 − 25 = 72
22. 64 − 23 = 41
23. 72 − 22 = 50
24. 89 − 55 = 34
25. 55 − 14 = 41

FITNESS FLASH: Clap your hands in front of your body as fast as you can for 30 seconds. Then, clap behind your back for 30 seconds. How many times can you clap each way?

47

Answer Key

Page 48 — Reading Comprehension

Use the information from the chart to find the answers.

Assignment Schedule

	Reading	Writing	Math	Science	S. Studies
Monday	unit 1	brainstorm	p. 21–22	plant seeds	none
Tuesday	unit 2	rough draft	p. 23–24	none	finish map
Wednesday	unit 3	edit	p. 25–26	record growth	none
Thursday	unit 4	revision	p. 27–28	none	time line
Friday	none	final draft	line graph	record growth	none

1. What assignment is due Wednesday in Science? __record growth__
2. What assignment is due Thursday in Writing? __revision__
3. On what day is the time line due in Social Studies? __Thursday__
4. In what subject is the assignment to complete pages 27–28 for Thursday? __Math__
5. What assignment is due Monday in Social Studies? __none__
6. On what day is unit 2 due in Reading? __Tuesday__
7. On what day is the line graph due in Math? __Friday__
8. What assignment is due Tuesday in Writing? __rough draft__
9. On what day are no assignments due in two classes? __Friday__

CHARACTER CHECK: Which school subject is hardest for you? What can you do to improve at it during the next school year?

48

Page 49 — Geometry

Name each shape.

1. pentagon
2. triangle
3. hexagon
4. rectangle
5. triangle
6. square
7. rectangle
8. circle

Circle the shape named. Then, answer the questions.

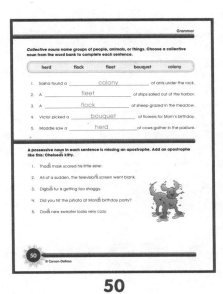

9. square pyramid
10. cube
11. sphere

12. Which shape has 6 equal faces? __cube__
13. Which shape is completely round and 3-D? __sphere__
14. Which shape has 2 pairs of equal sides? __rectangle__
15. Which shape has 5 total angles? __pentagon__

49

Page 50 — Grammar

Collective nouns name groups of people, animals, or things. Choose a collective noun from the word bank to complete each sentence.

herd	flock	fleet	bouquet	colony

1. Sasha found a __colony__ of ants under the rock.
2. A __fleet__ of ships sailed out of the harbor.
3. A __flock__ of sheep grazed in the meadow.
4. Victor picked a __bouquet__ of flowers for Mom's birthday.
5. Maddie saw a __herd__ of cows gather in the pasture.

A possessive noun in each sentence is missing an apostrophe. Add an apostrophe like this: Chelsea's kitty.

1. Thad's mask scared his little sister.
2. All of a sudden, the television's screen went blank.
3. Digby's fur is getting too shaggy.
4. Did you hit the piñata at Maria's birthday party?
5. Dad's new sweater looks very cozy.

50

Page 51 — Numbers & Place Value

Count 3-digit numbers by 1.
1. Start at 430.
   430, 431, 432, __433__, 434, __435__, __436__, 437
2. Start at 215.
   215, 216, __217__, 218, __219__, 220, __221__, 222

Skip count 3-digit numbers.
3. Count by 5. Start at 500.
   500, 505, __510__, __515__, 520, 525, 530, __535__
4. Count by 5. Start at 680.
   680, __685__, 690, __695__, 700, 705, __710__, __715__
5. Count by 10. Start at 200.
   200, __210__, __220__, 230, __240__, 250, __260__, 270
6. Count by 10. Start at 350.
   350, __360__, 370, __380__, __390__, 400, __410__, __420__
7. Count by 100. Start at 100.
   100, __200__, 300, __400__, __500__, 600, __700__
8. Count backward by 100. Start at 800.
   800, 700, __600__, __500__, 400, __300__, __200__

FITNESS FLASH: Walk from your room to your front door. Count how many steps it takes you to get there.

51

Page 52 — Reading Comprehension

Read the passage. Then, answer the questions.

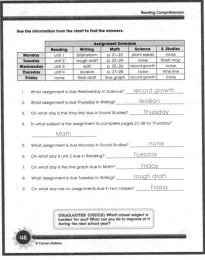

Birds make nests in many places. Woodpeckers make nests in tree trunks. Crows build them in high branches. A quail digs a shallow hole under a bush for a nest. Some desert owls build nests inside cacti. Swallows build mud nests under bridges. Wherever they live, birds find safe places to raise their babies.

1. Name four places birds can make nests.
   __in tree trunks__   __under bushes__
   __in high branches__   __inside cacti__
   __under bridges__
2. Why do birds make nests?
   __Bird make nests so that they have safe places__
   __to raise their babies.__
3. Where do woodpeckers build their nests?
   __in tree trunks__
4. What kind of bird builds mud nests under bridges?
   __swallows__
5. What kind of bird builds a nest in a cactus?
   __desert owl__
6. Where do quails build their nests?
   __in shallow holes under bushes__

FITNESS FLASH: Do 10 jumping jacks. Clap your hands above your head each time.

52

Page 55 — Time

Write the time two ways. The first one is done for you.

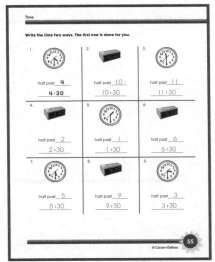

1. half past __4__   __4:30__
2. half past __10__   __10:30__
3. half past __11__   __11:30__
4. half past __2__   __2:30__
5. half past __1__   __1:30__
6. half past __6__   __6:30__
7. half past __5__   __5:30__
8. half past __9__   __9:30__
9. half past __3__   __3:30__

55

Answer Key

Page 56

Reading Comprehension

Use the context clues to make the best choice for each bold word's meaning.

1. Most small children are **forbidden** to cross the street without an adult.
   A. helped   B. told not to   C. forced
2. Tracy buttoned her **cardigan** to keep warm at the game.
   A. sweater   B. pajamas   C. boots
3. The autumn morning **dew** left the playground damp.
   A. clumps of dirt   B. pieces of ice   C. drops of water
4. Dad likes to **relax** on the sofa after he takes us swimming.
   A. jump   B. rest   C. eat
5. Our team must be **unified** if we want to win the championship.
   A. working together   B. awake   C. dressed up
6. I remember that type of butterfly by its **distinct** markings.
   A. yellow   B. special   C. dirty
7. The balloon **burst** as it brushed against the brick wall.
   A. flew higher   B. got away   C. popped
8. Some American Indians made the caves their **dwellings**.
   A. shoes   B. blankets   C. homes

FACTOID: Koalas sleep for up to 18 hours a day

56 © Carson-Dellosa

56

Page 57

Measurement & Data

Write the length of each object in centimeters.

1. 17 centimeters
2. 8 centimeters
3. (FLOSS) 4 centimeters
4. 6 centimeters
5. 9 centimeters
6. (SOAP) 7 centimeters

57 © Carson-Dellosa

57

Page 58

Reading Comprehension/Writing

Read the sentence pairs. Write an X beside the sentence that happens first.

1. X I planted seeds.
   ___ The garden grew.
2. X Noah got on his bike.
   ___ Noah rode his bike.
3. ___ I put on my shoes.
   X I put on my pants.
4. X We ate our dinner.
   ___ We washed the dishes.
5. X I brushed my teeth.
   ___ I put toothpaste on my toothbrush.
6. X I climbed into bed.
   ___ I fell asleep.

Is there anything at your school that you think should be changed? Write a letter to your principal or teacher explaining your opinion. Include good reasons to support your opinion.

Answers will vary.

58 © Carson-Dellosa

58

Page 59

Subtraction/Fitness

Subtract to solve each problem. Regroup if necessary.

1. 36 − 17 = 19
2. 98 − 19 = 79
3. 28 − 9 = 19
4. 41 − 15 = 26
5. 33 − 17 = 16
6. 72 − 53 = 19
7. 85 − 27 = 58
8. 43 − 29 = 14
9. 96 − 37 = 59
10. 64 − 36 = 28
11. 47 − 19 = 28
12. 94 − 26 = 68
13. 75 − 39 = 36
14. 61 − 22 = 39
15. 33 − 19 = 14
16. 71 − 46 = 25
17. 86 − 47 = 39
18. 94 − 35 = 59
19. 65 − 27 = 38
20. 92 − 44 = 48
21. 76 − 38 = 38
22. 64 − 35 = 29
23. 76 − 27 = 49
24. 52 − 44 = 8
25. 83 − 25 = 58

Bottle Bowling

Line up some empty plastic bottles on a wall. Stand a few feet away. Throw balls at the bottles and count how many times you throw before you hit all of them. Keep trying until the number of throws goes down.

Gather some balls near a sidewalk. Draw a chalk line and stand on it. Throw a ball as far away as you can. Ask a friend to put a stick on the spot where the ball landed. Do this several times, and then measure your longest throw.

© Carson-Dellosa 59

59

Page 60

Vocabulary/Grammar

Underline the root word in each word below. Then, write the definition of the word.

| un = not | dia = not, opposite of |
| re = again | pre = before |

1. dis**appear** = opposite of appear
2. re**fill** = fill again
3. un**lucky** = not lucky
4. dis**loyal** = not loyal
5. pre**pay** = pay before
6. un**worthy** = not worthy
7. re**write** = write again
8. pre**wash** = wash before

Reflexive pronouns are special pronouns that end with –self or –selves. Circle the reflexive pronoun in each sentence.

9. I told (myself) that we would stay dry, even if it rained.
10. The children were pleased with (themselves) for doing all their chores.
11. Grace made (herself) a tasty sandwich.
12. The kitten startled (itself) when it looked in the mirror.
13. After working all week, Ms. Chung gave (herself) the day off.
14. Did you give (yourself) a bath?

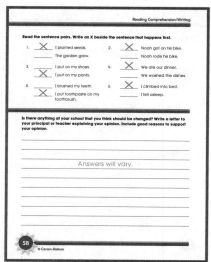

60 © Carson-Dellosa

60

Page 61

Time

Read the time on the first clock. Write the same time on the second clock.

1. 6:45
2. 5:15
3. 7:45
4. 11:15
5. 3:45
6. 10:15

FITNESS FLASH: Make up a silly walk. What is the silliest way you can walk from your room to the front door?

© Carson-Dellosa 61

61

Answer Key

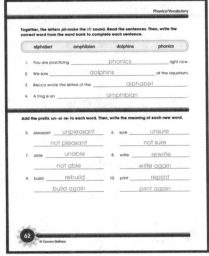

Page 62 — Phonics/Vocabulary

Together, the letters *ph* make the /f/ sound. Read the sentences. Then, write the correct word from the word bank to complete each sentence.

alphabet	amphibian	dolphins	phonics

1. You are practicing ___phonics___ right now.
2. We saw ___dolphins___ at the aquarium.
3. Becca wrote the letters of the ___alphabet___.
4. A frog is an ___amphibian___.

Add the prefix *un-* or *re-* to each word. Then, write the meaning of each new word.

5. pleasant — unpleasant — not pleasant
6. sure — unsure — not sure
7. able — unable — not able
8. write — rewrite — write again
9. build — rebuild — build again
10. print — reprint — print again

62

Page 63 — Addition & Subtraction

Use addition or subtraction to solve each problem.

1. Anthony made 9 clay pots. He broke 4 of the pots. How many pots does he have left? — 5 pots
2. Keenan had 17 boxes of candy to sell. He sold 2 boxes to his grandma. His dad sold 9 boxes to people at work. How many more boxes did Keenan have to sell? — 6 boxes
3. Min collects trading cards. She wants to collect all 15 cards in a series. She already has 8 of the cards. How many more cards does Min need? — 7 cards
4. Trina had 7 fish in her aquarium. She bought 4 more fish. How many fish does she have altogether? — 11 fish
5. Nina got 16 pieces of candy from the piñata. She ate 7 pieces. How many does she have left? — 9 pieces
6. Bradley read 5 books the first month of summer break and 8 books the second month. How many books did he read in all? — 13 books

FACTOID: The coldest temperature ever measured on Earth is -135.8 degrees Fahrenheit in Antarctica.

63

Page 64 — Reading Comprehension

A Sunny Flower

Use details from the passage to complete the puzzle. If you are unsure of a word's meaning, use context clues to help you.

The sunflower grows from a seed. First, a sunflower plant begins to grow a strong taproot. Soon, the green stalk begins to grow toward the warmth of the sun. As the plant grows, it forms a bud that will someday become a flower. The plant faces the east as the sun rises in the morning. Then, it follows the sun across the sky until it is facing west when the sun sets. As the flower's bud blooms, it unfolds into large, golden petals. The center of the flower is full of seeds. The seeds are either eaten or planted so that more sunflowers can grow.

Down
1. This passage is about the _____.
4. The bud _____ into a flower.
5. The _____ is like a stem.

Across
1. A sunflower grows toward the _____.
2. Seeds grow in the _____ of the flower.
3. Sunflowers have large, golden _____.
4. The plant forms a _____ that will become a flower.
6. The _____ begins to grow from the seed into the soil.

64

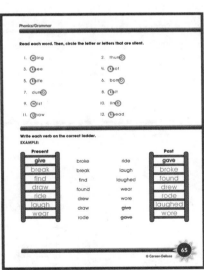

Page 65 — Phonics/Grammar

Read each word. Then, circle the letter or letters that are silent.

1. (w)ing
2. thum(b)
3. (k)nee
4. (k)not
5. (k)nife
6. bom(b)
7. dum(b)
8. (k)nit
9. (w)rist
10. lim(b)
11. (g)naw
12. (h)ead

Write each verb on the correct ladder.

EXAMPLE:

Present
- give
- break
- find
- draw
- ride
- laugh
- wear

broke — ride
break — laugh
find — laughed
found — wear
drew — wore
draw — rode
rode — give

Past
- gave
- broke
- found
- drew
- rode
- laughed
- wore

65

Page 70 — Social Studies Activity — BONUS

State Snatcher

The State Snatcher has stolen some of the abbreviations of the states. Write the missing abbreviations. Use another U.S. map to help you.

Postal Abbreviations Chart

Alabama AL	Indiana IN	Nebraska NE	South Carolina SC
Alaska AK	Iowa IA	Nevada NV	South Dakota SD
Arizona AZ	Kansas KS	New Hampshire NH	Tennessee TN
Arkansas AR	Kentucky KY	New Jersey NJ	Texas TX
California CA	Louisiana LA	New Mexico NM	Utah UT
Colorado CO	Maine ME	New York NY	Vermont VT
Connecticut CT	Maryland MD	North Carolina NC	Virginia VA
Delaware DE	Massachusetts MA	North Dakota ND	Washington WA
Florida FL	Michigan MI	Ohio OH	West Virginia WV
Georgia GA	Minnesota MN	Oklahoma OK	Wisconsin WI
Hawaii HI	Mississippi MS	Oregon OR	Wyoming WY
Idaho ID	Missouri MO	Pennsylvania PA	
Illinois IL	Montana MT	Rhode Island RI	

70

Page 75 — Social Studies Activity — BONUS

Color My World

Is it a city, state, country, continent or body of water? Color each box according to the Color Key. Use an atlas for help.

Color Key

city—orange	state—green	country—yellow
water—blue	continent—purple	

Atlantic Ocean	India	Colorado	Miami
Peru	Antarctica	Lake Michigan	Hawaii
New Orleans	Spain	Europe	Gulf of Mexico
Vermont	Phoenix	Japan	Paris
East China Sea	Egypt	Wyoming	Sweden
Africa	London	Hudson Bay	Connecticut
Greece	Minnesota	South America	Dallas
Oakland	Great Salt Lake	Argentina	Arctic Ocean
North America	Canada	Chicago	Arkansas
Lake Victoria	Iowa	Asia	Venezuela
Lima	Persian Gulf	Mexico	Moscow
Pacific Ocean	Maryland	Cincinnati	Brazil

75

Answer Key

Add to solve each problem.

1. Mischa has 9 [dog]. Uma has 12 [dog]. Quinton has 26 [dog].
   How many [dog] do they have in all? __47__

2. The toy store sold 12 [toy] in April,
   15 [toy] in May, and 20 [toy] in June.
   How many [toy] did the toy store sell in all? __47__

3. Geneva puts 6 [toy], 19 [toy], and
   29 [toy] on shelves. How many toys
   does Geneva put on shelves? __54__

4. The toy store has 31 [toy], 16 [toy],
   and 26 [toy]. How many of these toys
   does the toy store have in all? __73__

5. The bakery sells 12 [cupcake] on Thursday, 22
   on Friday, and 31 [cupcake] on Saturday.
   How many [cupcake] did the bakery sell? __65__

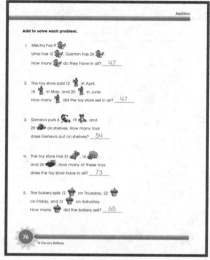

76

Draw a line to match each present-tense verb with its past-tense form.

1. freeze — held
2. hold — fell
3. catch — spoke
4. run — bought
5. speak — froze
6. fall — caught
7. buy — ran

Rewrite each set of underlined words using a possessive noun. The first one is done for you.

8. The book belonging to Connor is on the shelf. **Connor's book**

9. Have you seen the basketball belonging to Ivan? Ivan's basketball

10. I forgot to bring the snorkel belonging to Tiffany. Tiffany's snorkel

11. The pie plates belonging to Grandma are in the basement. Grandma's pie plates

12. The ballet shoes belonging to Chandra are too small. Chandra's ballet shoes

13. Halley left the tennis racquet belonging to Morgan on the bus. Morgan's tennis racquet

77

Practice "counting on" using the coins shown.

1. 25¢ 50¢ 60¢ 70¢ 80¢ 90¢ 95¢ 100¢ Total 100¢

2. 50¢ 60¢ 65¢ 70¢ 75¢ 76¢ 77¢ 78¢ Total 78¢

3. 50¢ 60¢ 70¢ 80¢ 85¢ 90¢ 91¢ 92¢ Total 92¢

4. 25¢ 50¢ 60¢ 65¢ 70¢ 75¢ 76¢ 77¢ Total 77¢

5. 50¢ 75¢ 80¢ 85¢ 86¢ 87¢ 88¢ 89¢ Total 89¢

6. 25¢ 50¢ 75¢ 85¢ 90¢ 95¢ 100¢ 101¢ Total 101¢

FITNESS FLASH: Find a soft surface and do five somersaults.

78

Read the passage. Then, answer the questions.

Some people save stamps. They keep their stamps in albums. They like to look at them. Some people like stamps that are very old. Some people like pretty stamps. Some people like stamps from places that are far away. Some stamps are worth a lot of money. Stamps that were printed incorrectly can be worth the most.

1. Where do some people keep their stamps?
   in albums

2. What is one reason people keep stamps?
   Answers may vary. Sample responses: They like to look at them. OR The stamps are worth a lot of money.

3. Name two kinds of stamps that people keep.
   Any two of the following: very old stamps, pretty stamps, stamps from far away places, stamps printed incorrectly

4. What kinds of stamps can be worth the most?
   stamps that were printed incorrectly

CHARACTER CHECK: What would you do if you heard your classmates teasing or making fun of someone?

79

Create a line plot using the length of each shape.

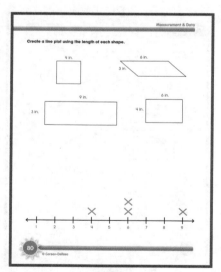

80

Read the sentences. Look at each underlined word. Then, color in the circle to tell if the word is spelled correctly or incorrectly.

EXAMPLE:

	CORRECT	INCORRECT
We ate biscuits with butter on them.	●	○
1. We wint to the store for some cereal and milk.	○	●
2. The cat will chase a mouse.	●	○
3. We will plant our flower bed.	●	○
4. The keng asked the queen to dance.	○	●
5. Think of a good name for a puppy.	●	○

Imagine that you are collecting items for a time capsule that will be opened in 20 years. What things would you put in the capsule to tell about your life right now?

Answers will vary.

81

Answer Key

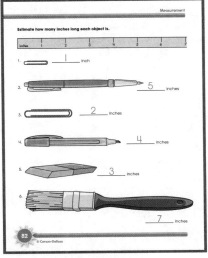

82

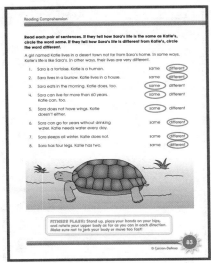

83

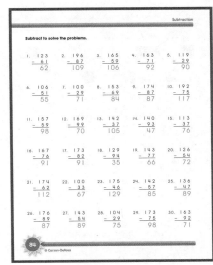

84

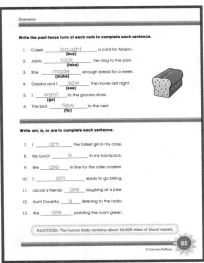

85

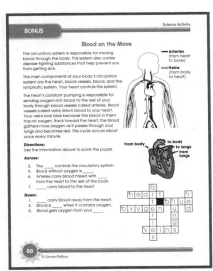

88

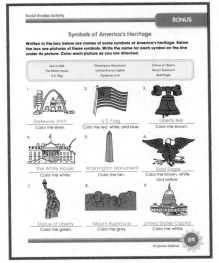

89

Answer Key

Page 91

Study the shapes. Then, answer each question.

square · rectangle · trapezoid · rhombus · circle
triangle · pentagon · hexagon · octagon

1. Which shapes are quadrilaterals (shapes with four sides)?
   square — trapezoid
   rectangle — rhombus
2. Name a quadrilateral with four equal sides. square or rhombus
3. What shape has three sides and three angles? triangle
4. What shape has no sides? circle
5. What shape has five sides? pentagon
6. What shape has six sides? hexagon
7. What shape has eight sides? octagon
8. What shapes have two or more parallel sides?
   square — rhombus
   rectangle — hexagon
   trapezoid — octagon
9. How is a trapezoid different from a rhombus? A trapezoid has only 2 equal sides and 1 set of parallel sides, but a rhombus has 4 equal sides and 2 sets of parallel sides.

91

Page 93

Use the passage to answer the questions.

1. Circle the letter of the sentence that tells the main idea.
   A. The ostrich is the largest bird.
   (B) The ostrich is one of the most unique of all birds.
   C. The ostrich lays eggs and has feathers like other birds.

2. Write a T if the sentence is true. Write an F if the sentence is false.
   F A. The ostrich can fly.
   T B. The ostrich can run very fast.
   T C. The mother ostrich lays its eggs in a hole in the ground.
   F D. The ostrich cannot kick without falling down.

3. Compare the ostrich to other birds. Put an X in the boxes to show whether each characteristic describes the ostrich, other birds, or both.

ostrich		other birds
☐	can fly	☒
☒	has/have feathers	☒
☒	lays eggs	☒
☒	grows to be 8 feet tall	☐
☒	protective of young	☐

4. Complete each sentence by circling the correct homophone.
   The ostrich can grow to be ____ feet tall. ate (eight)
   The ostrich can weigh more than ____ hundred pounds. too (two)
   The ostrich egg can nearly three pounds. way (weigh)
   The ____ ostrich digs a hole in the ground for the nest. mail (male)

The ending -er sometimes means "more." It may be used to compare two things. The ending -est means "most." It is used to compare more than two things. If a word ends in e, only add -r or -st to the word. Write the appropriate ending in each blank.

5. The ostrich is large r than most birds.
6. It is probably the tall est of all birds.
7. Ostrich eggs are the larg est eggs in the world.
8. Its powerful legs make it the fast est bird on the ground.

93

Page 94

What fraction of each figure is shaded?

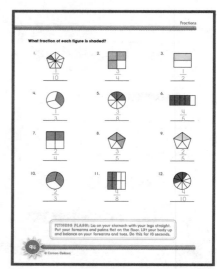

1. 1/10
2. 3/4
3. 1/2
4. 1/3
5. 3/8
6. 4/5
7. 2/4
8. 3/5
9. 2/5
10. 2/3
11. 4/8
12. 4/10

FITNESS FLASH: Lie on your stomach with your legs straight. Put your forearms and palms flat on the floor. Lift your body up and balance on your forearms and toes. Do this for 10 seconds.

94

Page 95

Solve each problem.

1. The small hand is between 5 and 6.
   The large hand is on the 9.
   The time is 5:45.

2. The small hand is between 3 and 4.
   The large hand is on the 6.
   The time is 3:30.

3. The small hand is on the 8.
   The large hand is on the 12.
   The time is 8:00.

4. The small hand is on the 4.
   The large hand is on the 12.
   The time is 4:00.

5. The small hand is between 10 and 11.
   The large hand is on the 3.
   The time is 10:15.

95

Page 96

Look at each underlined word. On the line, write whether it is a noun, pronoun, verb, adjective, or adverb.

1. noun — The old blue tent smelled of leaves and woody air.
2. adverb — Dad carefully unzipped the tent's windows.
3. adjective — The smell of crispy bacon filled the air.
4. verb — A clear stream ran along one side of the campsite.
5. pronoun — I couldn't wait to start the campfire.
6. verb — We roasted hot dogs and marshmallows.

Add the missing commas to each address below. Use this symbol to add them: ⌄.

7. 81 Riverbrook Rd.
   Grand Rapids, MI 49505
8. 132 West Billingsley Lane
   Taos, NM 87571
9. 1425 Newman Terrace
   Des Moines, IA 50328
10. 21896 Landon Blvd.
    Orlando, FL 32807
11. 10346 State Route 39
    Tuscaloosa, AL 35401
12. 992 Rabbit Run Rd.
    Champaign, IL 61826

CHARACTER CHECK: Have you made any promises to friends or family members lately? What are some ways you can take responsibility and keep your word to them?

96

Page 97

Add to solve each problem.

1. 182 + 703 = 885
2. 231 + 547 = 778
3. 825 + 163 = 988
4. 436 + 562 = 998
5. 325 + 202 = 527

6. 274 + 320 = 594
7. 641 + 345 = 986
8. 908 + 61 = 969
9. 365 + 424 = 789
10. 207 + 712 = 919

11. 352 + 436 = 788
12. 475 + 510 = 985
13. 724 + 143 = 867
14. 650 + 227 = 877
15. 298 + 500 = 798

16. 525 + 261 = 788
17. 631 + 155 = 786
18. 447 + 432 = 879
19. 319 + 450 = 769
20. 752 + 136 = 888

21. 933 + 52 = 985
22. 547 + 131 = 678
23. 830 + 69 = 899
24. 626 + 331 = 957
25. 487 + 411 = 898

26. 631 + 325 = 956
27. 488 + 211 = 699
28. 562 + 407 = 969
29. 723 + 166 = 889
30. 506 + 353 = 859

FITNESS FLASH: Jump up and down in one spot for 30 seconds. How high can you go?

97

Answer Key

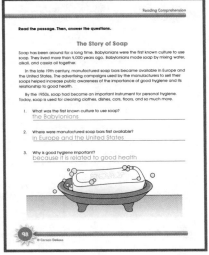

98

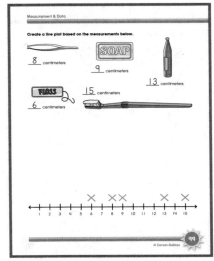

99

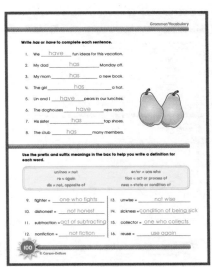

100

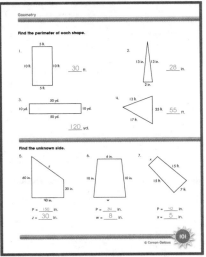

101

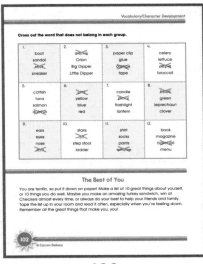

102

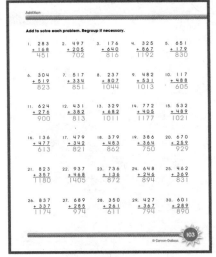

103

Answer Key

Page 104

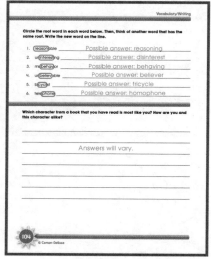

Circle the root word in each word below. Then, think of another word that has the same root. Write the new word on the line.

1. reasonable — Possible answer: reasoning
2. uninteresting — Possible answer: disinterest
3. misbehavior — Possible answer: behaving
4. unbelievable — Possible answer: believer
5. bicycle — Possible answer: tricycle
6. telephone — Possible answer: homophone

Which character from a book that you have read is most like you? How are you and this character alike?

Answers will vary.

Page 105

Time

Write each time two ways.

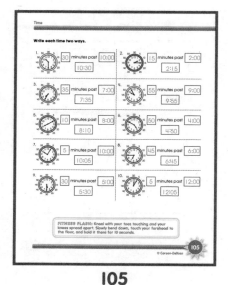

1. 30 minutes past 10:00 — 10:30
2. 15 minutes past 2:00 — 2:15
3. 35 minutes past 7:00 — 7:35
4. 55 minutes past 9:00 — 9:55
5. 10 minutes past 8:00 — 8:10
6. 50 minutes past 4:00 — 4:50
7. 5 minutes past 10:00 — 10:05
8. 45 minutes past 6:00 — 6:45
9. 30 minutes past 5:00 — 5:30
10. 5 minutes past 12:00 — 12:05

FITNESS FLASH: Kneel with your toes touching and your knees spread apart. Slowly bend down, touch your forehead to the floor, and hold it there for 10 seconds.

Page 108

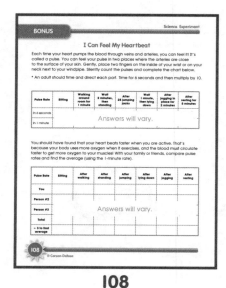

I Can Feel My Heartbeat

Each time your heart pumps the blood through veins and arteries, you can feel it! It's called a pulse. You can feel your pulse in two places where the arteries are close to the surface of your skin. Gently, place two fingers on the inside of your wrist or on your neck next to your windpipe. Silently count the pulses and complete the chart below.

*An adult should time and direct each part. Time for 6 seconds and then multiply by 10.

Answers will vary.

You should have found that your heart beats faster when you are active. That's because your body uses more oxygen when it exercises, and the blood must circulate faster to get more oxygen to your muscles! With your family or friends, compare pulse rates and find the average (using the 1-minute rate).

Answers will vary.

Page 109

Social Studies Activity — BONUS

Up the Lazy River

"The steamboat is coming!" was a cry heard in the many small river towns in the 1800s. Steamboats carried people and packages along the waterways before the faster railroads were developed.

The shipping tags below tell where each package is beginning and ending its journey. Use a map, atlas, or other reference book to find the river on which the steamboat will be traveling. Some steamboats may have to travel on more than one river.

Directions: Write the name of the river routes on each shipping tag.

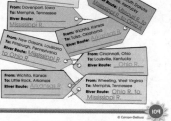

From: Omaha, Nebraska To: Great Falls, Montana River Route: Missouri R.

From: Pierre, South Dakota To: Louisville, Kentucky River Route: Missouri R. to Ohio R.

From: Davenport, Iowa To: Memphis, Tennessee River Route: Mississippi R.

From: Wichita, Kansas To: Tulsa, Oklahoma River Route: Arkansas R.

From: New Orleans, Louisiana To: Pittsburgh, Pennsylvania River Route: Mississippi R. to Ohio R.

From: Cincinnati, Ohio To: Louisville, Kentucky River Route: Ohio R.

From: Wichita, Kansas To: Little Rock, Arkansas River Route: Arkansas R.

From: Wheeling, West Virginia To: Memphis, Tennessee River Route: Ohio R. to Mississippi R.

Page 111

Reading Comprehension

The Midnight Ride

Number the sentences 1–6 to retell the story below in sequence.

It was early morning on April 19, 1775. Paul Revere and many other colonists were ready to fight against the British army. They called themselves *minutemen* because they would need to be ready to fight at a minute's notice. First, Paul waited for a signal from the American spies. They knew the British army would eventually move toward Lexington and Concord, but they did not know whether the British would travel by land or across the water. When the spies told Paul, he would send a signal to the other minutemen, telling them from which direction the British were attacking. Next, he would ride his horse quickly through the farmland and towns, shouting the news that the British were coming.

At last, the word came from the spies. Paul immediately ordered two lanterns to be hung in the tall tower of the church, a signal that meant the British were attacking by sea. Then, he mounted his horse and rode fast into the night. Paul Revere knew the importance of warning the minutemen to prepare for battle. The British army had more men and more guns, so the minutemen would need to surprise them. Paul rode through Lexington, shouting the news. But, as he rode out of town, he was caught by the British. Meanwhile, two other riders made it further and told the minutemen to be ready to fight in Concord.

Soon, the British army reached Concord. They had no idea that the minutemen were waiting. They were surprised and fled the area. The minutemen that were awakened had won their first fight.

4 Paul Revere was caught by a British soldier.

2 Two lanterns were lit in the church tower.

3 Paul Revere rode through Lexington.

6 The minutemen surprised the British army in Concord.

1 Paul Revere received word from the spies.

5 Two other American riders warned the minutemen to gather in Concord.

Page 112

Subtraction/Fitness

Subtract to solve each problem.

1. 684 − 253 = 431
2. 634 − 421 = 213
3. 835 − 610 = 225
4. 738 − 502 = 236
5. 325 − 102 = 223

6. 874 − 321 = 553
7. 647 − 325 = 322
8. 958 − 146 = 812
9. 363 − 242 = 121
10. 567 − 362 = 205

11. 283 − 220 = 63
12. 488 − 351 = 137
13. 695 − 233 = 462
14. 719 − 305 = 414
15. 894 − 752 = 142

16. 975 − 342 = 633
17. 767 − 425 = 342
18. 836 − 132 = 704
19. 547 − 235 = 312
20. 658 − 510 = 148

21. 393 − 173 = 220
22. 649 − 235 = 414
23. 786 − 526 = 260
24. 999 − 683 = 316
25. 887 − 346 = 541

Jump and Sing

Grab a jump rope if you have one, or borrow one from a friend. As you are jumping, sing one of your favorite songs. Try to keep jumping rope without stumbling until you finish the song. As you get better, try singing longer songs. Have a friend time you to see how long you can jump. If you have friends who like to jump rope, too, you could even put on a jump-rope concert!

Answer Key

113

Vocabulary

Add the suffixes *-ed* and *-ing* to each base word. You may need to drop letters from or add letters to some words before adding the suffixes.

1. fake	2. jump	3. kiss	4. cook	5. grate
faked	jumped	kissed	cooked	grated
faking	jumping	kissing	cooking	grating
6. wrap	7. snooze	8. pop	9. talk	10. grin
wrapped	snoozed	popped	talked	grinned
wrapping	snoozing	popping	talking	grinning

Write the letter of the correct definition next to each word.

1. C cheerful — A. ready to help
2. E hopeless — B. without sun
3. D doubtful — C. very cheery
4. B sunless — D. having doubts
5. A helpful — E. without hope

114

Measurement

Estimate how many centimeters long each object is.

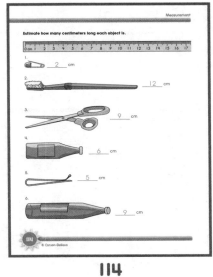

1. 2 cm
2. 12 cm
3. 9 cm
4. 6 cm
5. 5 cm
6. 9 cm

115

Money

Solve each problem. The first one is done for you.

1. Maurice had 3 dimes.
   He found 5 pennies in the couch cushions.
   How much money does Maurice have now? **35¢**

2. Trisha has 3 nickels.
   Brandi has 11 pennies.
   How much money do they have altogether? 26¢

3. Addie has 1 dime and 7 pennies.
   How much money does she have? 17¢

4. Ashton pulls 2 one-dollar bills, 1 quarter, 1 dime, 3 nickels, and 9 pennies from his piggy bank.
   How much money does Ashton have? $2.59

5. Bailey's mother put a one-dollar bill, 2 quarters, 3 dimes, 1 nickel, and 7 pennies in an envelope for Bailey to use at the county fair.
   How much money did Bailey's mother give her for the county fair? $1.92

117

Reading Comprehension

Use the passage to answer the questions.

1. Why is it important to obey bicycle safety rules?
   because bicycle accidents can be very serious

2. When should you wear bright clothing?
   A. during the day
   B. during the evening
   C. every time you ride
   D. never

3. What parts on the bicycle should you check before riding?
   tires, brakes, handlebars, and pedals

4. What safety equipment should you use when you ride?
   reflectors, bicycle helmet, bright clothing, and laced shoes

5. On which side of the street should you ride your bike?
   A. with the direction of traffic
   B. the left side
   C. on the sidewalk
   D. doesn't matter where

6. When riding your bike, how should you notify others that you will be turning?
   with arm signals

118

Subtraction/Character Development

Subtract to solve each problem. Regroup if necessary.

1. 837 − 138 = 699
2. 516 − 247 = 269
3. 825 − 356 = 469
4. 713 − 284 = 429
5. 624 − 367 = 257
6. 283 − 96 = 187
7. 567 − 275 = 292
8. 928 − 189 = 739
9. 785 − 496 = 289
10. 497 − 269 = 228
11. 553 − 129 = 424
12. 476 − 138 = 338
13. 764 − 335 = 429
14. 676 − 227 = 449
15. 952 − 344 = 608
16. 837 − 253 = 584
17. 689 − 496 = 193
18. 941 − 250 = 691
19. 277 − 193 = 84
20. 765 − 295 = 470

Boredom Busters

Feeling bored this summer? Instead of complaining or moping, here's another solution: Make a Boredom Buster list for those times when it seems like there's nothing to do. First, pick a letter of the alphabet. Then, list ten things you wish you were doing that start with that letter. Finally, pick the best thing on the list and do it. Save your list for the next time you are bored or make a new one with a new letter.

119

Grammar

Write the word *went* or *gone* to complete each sentence. Remember: The word *gone* needs another word to help it, such as *has* or *have*.

1. Carlos went to the park after school.
2. Kami has gone shopping for new shoes.
3. Ebony went with Byron to play.
4. We will be gone on vacation all week.
5. My father went to work this evening.

Write a word from each box to complete each sentence.

6. The car will stop
   The car is stopping
   The car has stopped
   (stop / stopped / stopping)

7. The baby can crawl
   The baby is crawling
   The baby crawled
   (crawl / crawled / crawling)

8. The kangaroo is hopping
   The kangaroo hopped
   The kangaroo can hop
   (hop / hopped / hopping)

Answer Key

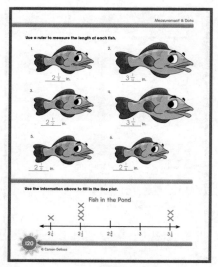

Page 120

Measurement & Data

Use a ruler to measure the length of each fish.

1. $2\frac{1}{2}$ in.
2. $3\frac{1}{4}$ in.
3. $2\frac{1}{2}$ in.
4. $3\frac{1}{4}$ in.
5. $2\frac{1}{2}$ in.
6. $3\frac{1}{4}$ in.

Use the information above to fill in the line plot.

Fish in the Pond

$2\frac{1}{4}$ $2\frac{1}{2}$ $2\frac{3}{4}$ 3 $3\frac{1}{4}$

120

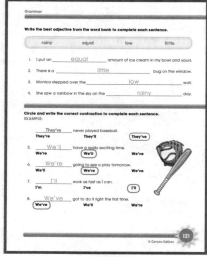

Page 121

Grammar

Write the best adjective from the word bank to complete each sentence.

| rainy | equal | low | little |

1. I put an _____equal_____ amount of ice cream in my bowl and yours.
2. There is a _____little_____ bug on the window.
3. Monica stepped over the _____low_____ wall.
4. She saw a rainbow in the sky on the _____rainy_____ day.

Circle and write the correct contraction to complete each sentence.
EXAMPLE:

_____They've_____ never played baseball.
They're   They'll   (They've)

5. _____We'll_____ have a really exciting time.
We'll   (We'll)   We've
6. _____We're_____ going to see a play tomorrow.
We'll   (We're)   We've
7. _____I'll_____ work as fast as I can.
I'm   I've   (I'll)
8. _____We've_____ got to do it right the first time.
(We've)   We'll   We're

121

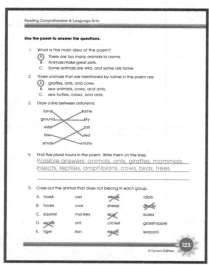

Page 123

Reading Comprehension & Language Arts

Use the poem to answer the questions.

1. What is the main idea of the poem?
   (A) There are too many animals to name.
   B. Animals make great pets.
   C. Some animals are wild, and some are tame.

2. Three animals that are mentioned by name in the poem are
   (A) giraffes, ants, and cows.
   B. sea animals, cows, and ants.
   C. sea turtles, crows, and ants.

3. Draw a line between antonyms.
   land — tame
   ground — sky
   wild — tall
   few — sea
   small — many

4. Find five plural nouns in the poem. Write them on the lines.
   Possible answers: animals, ants, giraffes, mammals, insects, reptiles, amphibians, cows, birds, trees

5. Cross out the animal that does not belong in each group.
   A. hawk   owl   ~~whale~~   robin
   B. horse   cow   sheep   ~~turtle~~
   C. squirrel   monkey   ~~seal~~   koala
   D. ~~snake~~   ant   cricket   grasshopper
   E. tiger   lion   ~~rabbit~~   leopard

123

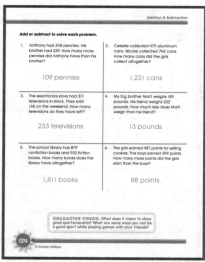

Page 124

Addition & Subtraction

Add or subtract to solve each problem.

1. Anthony had 348 pennies. His brother had 239. How many more pennies did Anthony have than his brother?

   109 pennies

2. Celeste collected 479 aluminum cans. Nicole collected 742 cans. How many cans did the girls collect altogether?

   1,221 cans

3. The electronics store had 371 televisions in stock. They sold 138 on the weekend. How many televisions do they have left?

   233 televisions

4. My big brother Matt weighs 189 pounds. His friend weighs 202 pounds. How much less does Matt weigh than his friend?

   13 pounds

5. The school library has 879 nonfiction books and 932 fiction books. How many books does the library have altogether?

   1,811 books

6. The girls earned 487 points for selling cookies. The boys earned 399 points. How many more points did the girls earn than the boys?

   88 points

CHARACTER CHECK: What does it mean to show good sportsmanship? What are some ways you can be a good sport while playing games with your friends?

124

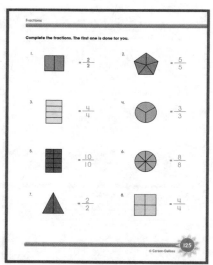

Page 125

Fractions

Complete the fractions. The first one is done for you.

1. = $\frac{2}{2}$
2. = $\frac{5}{5}$
3. = $\frac{4}{4}$
4. = $\frac{3}{3}$
5. = $\frac{10}{10}$
6. = $\frac{8}{8}$
7. = $\frac{2}{2}$
8. = $\frac{4}{4}$

125

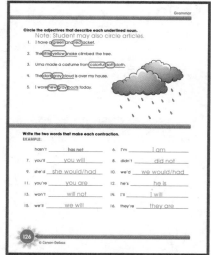

Page 126

Grammar

Circle the adjectives that describe each underlined noun.
Note: Student may also circle articles.
1. I have a (green) and (red) jacket.
2. The (little) (yellow) snake climbed the tree.
3. Uma made a costume from (colorful) (soft) cloth.
4. The (dark) (gray) cloud is over my house.
5. I wore (new) (gray) boots today.

Write the two words that make each contraction.
EXAMPLE:

6. hasn't _____has not_____
7. you'll _____you will_____
8. didn't _____did not_____
9. she'd _____she would/had_____
10. we'd _____we would/had_____
11. you're _____you are_____
12. he's _____he is_____
13. won't _____will not_____
14. I'll _____I will_____
15. we'll _____we will_____
16. they're _____they are_____

126

234

© Carson-Dellosa

Answer Key

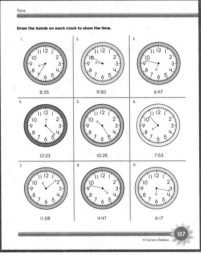

127

128

129

130

131

132

Answer Key

Complete the multiplication chart. Then, answer the questions.

x	1	2	3	4	5	6	7	8	9
1	1	2	3	4	5	6	7	8	9
2	2	4	6	8	10	12	14	16	18
3	3	6	9	12	15	18	21	24	27
4	4	8	12	16	20	24	28	32	36
5	5	10	15	20	25	30	35	40	45
6	6	12	18	24	30	36	42	48	54
7	7	14	21	28	35	42	49	56	63
8	8	16	24	32	40	48	56	64	72
9	9	18	27	36	45	54	63	72	81

1. What does any number times 1 equal? __itself__

2. What pattern do you see in the twos? __all even numbers__

3. What pattern do you see in the fives? __All numbers end in 5 or 0.__

4. Add the digits for each answer in the nines. What number does each answer equal? __9__

5. 3 × 4 = 12. What does 4 × 3 equal? __12__

133

Use the letter to answer the questions.

1. The word restricted means
   - A. tricked again
   - B. kept within limits ✓
   - C. yelled
   - D. upset

2. What was Ebony's punishment for not completing her chore?
   - A. cleaning her room
   - B. flying a kite
   - C. not playing outside ✓
   - D. cleaning the dishes

3. What feeling did Ebony get when she was able to fly her kite?
   - A. happy ✓
   - B. depressed
   - C. anxious
   - D. scared

4. What made Ebony's mother happy?
   - A. dinner
   - B. Ebony's red cheeks and smile ✓
   - C. Ebony's kite
   - D. gardening

5. Why do you think Ebony likes to see her mother smile?

   _____

   Answers will vary.

   _____

   _____

135

Find the product for each pair of factors below. Use the code to find the letters. Write the letters on the lines to answer the two riddles.

A	B	C	D	E	F	G	H	I	J	K	L	M	N	O	P	Q	R	S	T	U	V	W	X	Y	Z
64	42	27	24	16	0	18	40	11	5	49	25	12	13	21	56	8	54	32	28	45	60	9	14

How do you make the number *one* disappear?

A D D   T H E
8×8 9×3 3×9   9×6 2×9 3×8

L E T T E R   G
7×7 6×4 6×9 9×6 6×4 9×6   10×0

A N D   I T ' S
8×8 5×5 9×3   8×5 9×6 4×2

" G O N E "!
8×3 3×4 5×5 4×6

What can you hold in your left hand but not in your right hand?

Y O U R
3×3 6×2 8×4 7×8

R I G H T
8×7 8×1 1×0 6×3 6×9

E L B O W!
8×3 7×7 2×2 3×4 9×5

136

Adopt an Animal

The seas of the world are filled with an amazing variety of life. Starfish, crabs, flying fish, angelfish, worms, turtles, sharks and whales all make their homes underwater. The shape, color, and size of most sea animals depend on their lifestyles and where they live in the seas. Select a sea animal and become an expert on it. Research your animal and complete the profile below.

Common Name _____

Scientific Name _____

Description:

weight:

length: Answers will vary.

body shape:

tail shape:

color:

unusual characteristics:

Picture

Behaviors

Description of Habitat: _____

Food and Feeding Habits: _____

_____

Migration (if applicable): _____

140

What fraction of each figure is shaded? Compare the fractions. Use >, <, or =.

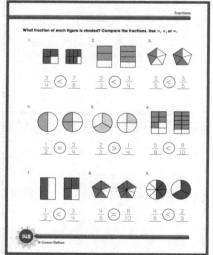

1. $\frac{3}{4}$ < $\frac{7}{8}$

2. $\frac{2}{3}$ < $\frac{3}{4}$

3. $\frac{2}{5}$ < $\frac{3}{5}$

4. $\frac{1}{2}$ = $\frac{2}{4}$

5. $\frac{2}{3}$ > $\frac{1}{4}$

6. $\frac{5}{8}$ < $\frac{8}{10}$

7. $\frac{1}{2}$ < $\frac{3}{4}$

8. $\frac{4}{5}$ = $\frac{8}{10}$

9. $\frac{4}{8}$ < $\frac{2}{3}$

148

Underline the verb that completes each sentence.

1. Colby and Zoe (are, is) going on a spring scavenger hunt.

2. Colby (spot, spots) leaves budding on a tree.

3. Zoe (see, sees) a robin searching for worms in the green grass.

4. A warm breeze (melt, melts) the last of the snow.

5. A kite (soar, soars) overhead.

6. Daffodils and tulips (bloom, blooms) in the garden.

7. The children (hear, hears) happy songbirds singing.

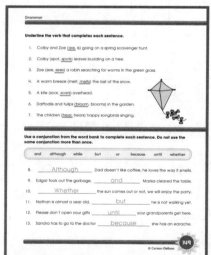

Use a conjunction from the word bank to complete each sentence. Do not use the same conjunction more than once.

and	although	while	but	or	because	until	whether

8. __Although__ Dad doesn't like coffee, he loves the way it smells.

9. Edgar took out the garbage, __and__ Marisa cleared the table.

10. __Whether__ the sun comes out or not, we will enjoy the party.

11. Nathan is almost a year old, __but__ he is not walking yet.

12. Please don't open your gifts __until__ your grandparents get here.

13. Sandra has to go to the doctor __because__ she has an earache.

149

236

© Carson-Dellosa

Answer Key

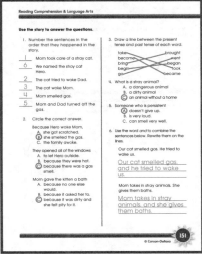

151 — Reading Comprehension & Language Arts

Use the story to answer the questions.

1. Number the sentences in the order that they happened in the story.
   - 1 Mom took care of a stray cat.
   - 6 We named the stray cat Hero.
   - 2 The cat tried to wake Dad.
   - 3 The cat woke Mom.
   - 4 Mom smelled gas.
   - 5 Mom and Dad turned off the gas.

2. Circle the correct answer.
   - Because Hero woke Mom,
     - A. she got scratched.
     - B. she smelled the gas.
     - C. the family awoke.
   - They opened all of the windows
     - A. to let Hero outside.
     - B. because they were hot.
     - C. because there was a gas smell.
   - Mom gave the kitten a bath
     - A. because no one else would.
     - B. because it asked her to.
     - C. because it was dirty and she felt pity for it.

3. Draw a line between the present tense and past tense of each word.
   - take — brought
   - become — went
   - bring — began
   - begin — took
   - go — became

4. What is a stray animal?
   - A. a dangerous animal
   - B. a dirty animal
   - C. an animal without a home

5. Someone who is persistent
   - A. doesn't give up.
   - B. is very loud.
   - C. can smell very well.

6. Use the word *and* to combine the sentences below. Rewrite them on the lines.
   - Our cat smelled gas. He tried to wake us.
     - Our cat smelled gas, and he tried to wake us.
   - Mom takes in stray animals. She gives them baths.
     - Mom takes in stray animals, and she gives them baths.

---

152 — Multiplication

Multiply to solve each problem.

1. 2 × 2 = 4
2. 3 × 2 = 6
3. 5 × 3 = 15
4. 1 × 6 = 6
5. 6 × 2 = 12
6. 2 × 8 = 16
7. 5 × 2 = 10
8. 2 × 6 = 12
9. 2 × 4 = 8
10. 2 × 1 = 2
11. 7 × 2 = 14
12. 3 × 6 = 18
13. 9 × 2 = 18
14. 8 × 2 = 16
15. 4 × 5 = 20
16. 3 × 9 = 27
17. 6 × 5 = 30
18. 4 × 6 = 24
19. 3 × 7 = 21
20. 8 × 3 = 24
21. 4 × 4 = 16
22. 5 × 6 = 30
23. 5 × 8 = 40
24. 7 × 9 = 63
25. 8 × 8 = 64
26. 5 × 4 = 20
27. 9 × 8 = 72
28. 6 × 7 = 42
29. 5 × 7 = 35
30. 4 × 8 = 32

---

153 — Multiplication

Multiply to solve each problem.

1. Jason has 4 bags. He puts 5 marbles in each bag. How many marbles are there in all?
   - Jason has __4__ bags.
   - Each bag has __5__ marbles.
   - There are __20__ marbles in all.

2. There are 4 pots of flowers. There are 2 flowers in each pot. How many flowers are there in all?
   - There are __4__ pots.
   - Each pot has __2__ flowers.
   - There are __8__ flowers in all.

3. Kami jumped over 4 rocks. She jumped over each rock 3 times. How many times did she jump in all?
   - There are __4__ rocks.
   - Kami jumped over each rock __3__ times.
   - She jumped __12__ times in all.

Write a word problem to fit the number sentence. Solve.

5 × 1 = __5__

Answers will vary.

---

154 — Vocabulary/Grammar

Add the ending shown to each base word to make a new word. Don't forget to change the spelling of the base word when the ending is added.

change y to i
1. fly + s = flies
2. happy + ness = happiness

double the final consonant
3. sip + ing = sipping
4. hop + ed = hopped

drop the final e
5. smile + ed = smiled
6. pile + ing = piled

change ie to y or y to ie
7. lie + ing = lying
8. kitty + s = kitties

Write N if the verb is in the present tense (happening now). Write P if the verb is in the past tense (already happened). Write F if the verb is in the future tense (will happen in the future).

9. F We will run later.
10. N I have a sandwich.
11. P Hugo ate a cucumber.
12. F We will go home soon.
13. N I love cucumbers!
14. N Neyla is playing soccer.
15. P I biked with my mom.
16. P Jarvis washed his dog.

FACTOID: When howler monkeys howl, they can be heard from up to 3 miles away.

---

155 — Geometry

Count the squares that make up each rectangle.

1. 12 equal squares
2. 9 equal squares
3. 8 equal squares

Draw same-size squares to fill each rectangle. Then, count the number of squares.

4. 10 square units
5. 12 square units
6. 4 square units
7. 16 square units
8. 12 square units
9. 20 square units

---

157 — Reading Comprehension

Use the passage to answer the questions.

1. What do newborn sea horses usually eat?
   - A. crabs
   - B. flowers
   - C. tiny sea animals
   - D. sand

2. What does it mean to "put a twist on" something?
   - to change it, maybe even to its opposite

3. Why do newborn sea horses rise to the surface of the water?
   - so that they can get air, which helps them stay upright

4. What word means "sea monster"?
   - A. kampos
   - B. phylum
   - C. hippos
   - D. genus

5. In your opinion, what is the most interesting thing about the sea horse?
   - Answers will vary.

CHARACTER CHECK: What do you complain about the most? What could you do about it instead of complaining?

Answer Key

Multiply to solve each problem.

1. Tripp wants to buy 6 pieces of bubblegum. Each piece costs 5 cents. How much will he have to pay for the bubblegum?

   Tripp wants to buy __6__ pieces of bubblegum.

   One piece of bubblegum costs __5__ cents.

   Tripp will have to pay __30__ cents total.

2. There are 7 girls on stage. Each girl is holding 8 flowers. How many flowers are there in all?

   There are __7__ girls.

   Each girl is holding __8__ flowers.

   There are __56__ flowers in all.

3. There are 3 rows of desks. There are 8 desks in each row. How many desks are there in all?

   There are __3__ rows of desks.

   There are __8__ desks in each row.

   There are __24__ desks in all.

Write a word problem to fit the number sentence. Solve.

8 x 4 = __32__

Answers will vary.

158

Read each scale. Write the measurement. Circle the best unit of measurement by using the weight chart below.

1 ounce	1 pound	1 gram	1 kilogram

1. __2__ (pounds) / ounces
2. __5__ grams / (pounds)
3. __26__ (kilograms) / ounces
4. __105__ grams / (pounds)
5. __38__ pounds / (ounces)
6. __22__ grams / (pounds)

FITNESS FLASH: Stretch a long piece of string in a straight line on the floor. Slowly walk heel-to-toe along the string. How far can you walk the "tightrope" without falling off?

159

Change each declarative sentence into an interrogative sentence.
EXAMPLE:

The busy delivery driver is leaving. __Is the busy delivery driver leaving?__

1. That woman is Grey's mother. __Is that woman Grey's mother?__

2. She can ride her new bike. __Can she ride her new bike?__

3. I will ride the brown horse. __Will I ride the brown horse?__

In a dictionary, guide words are at the top of each page. The guide word on the left tells the first word on the page. The guide word on the right tells the last word on the page. Circle the word that would be on the page with each set of guide words.

4. **pastor – penguin**
   panda   pig   (paw)

5. **match – monkey**
   (math)   magic   moss

6. **bean – buffalo**
   butter   bag   (bison)

7. **hammer – hark**
   hall   (hand)   hail

8. **rabbit – rock**
   (racer)   racket   radius

160

Make a mental computation first. Then, solve the problem.

1. Eight girls and 5 boys each have a button collection. Each girl has 8 buttons in her collection, and each boy has 4 buttons in his collection. How many buttons altogether do the boys and girls have?

   Mental Computation: Answers will vary.

   The boys and girls have __84__ buttons altogether.

2. There are 3 rows of 5 computers in each office. If there are 6 offices in the building, how many computers are in the building altogether?

   Mental Computation: Answers will vary.

   There are __90__ computers in the building.

3. Lucy bought 5 bags of dried mango slices. Each bag has 7 slices. How many mango slices does Lucy have left over after she gives away 10 slices?

   Mental Computation: Answers will vary.

   Lucy has __25__ mango slices left.

4. Ishmael bought 6 boxes of Mighty Mints and 5 boxes of Fudge Crunchies. Each Mighty Mints box has 10 cookies and each Fudge Crunchies box has 7. How many cookies does Ishmael have altogether?

   Mental Computation: Answers will vary.

   Ishmael has __95__ cookies altogether.

FITNESS FLASH: Lie on your back. With your knees bent, raise your legs and pump them back and forth like you are riding a bicycle. Do this for 60 seconds.

161

BONUS

Body Building Blocks

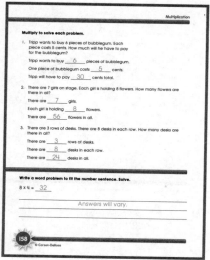

Just like some houses are built with bricks, your body is built with cells. Every part of your body is made of cells.

Cells differ in **size** and **shape**, but they all have a few things in common. All cells have a nucleus. The **nucleus** is the center of the cell. It controls the cell's activities.

Cells can **divide** and become two cells exactly like the original cell.

Your body has many kinds of cells. Each kind has a special job. **Muscle** cells help you move. **Nerve** cells carry messages between your brain and other parts of your body. Blood cells carry **oxygen** to other cells in your body.

Directions: Complete each sentence using the words in bold from above.

1. The __n u c l e u s__ controls the cell's activities.
                 3

2. Cells differ in __s i z e__ and __s h a p e__.
                    2   7

3. One cell can __d i v i d e__ into two cells.
                          6

4. __M u s c l e__ cells help you move.
            5

5. Blood cells carry __o x y g e n__ to other cells in your body.
                              4

Unscramble the numbered letters above to discover this amazing fact.

6. You began life as a __s i n g l e__ cell.
                        1 2 3 4 5 6

muscle cell

nerve cell

nucleus

blood cells

163

BONUS

North, South, East, and West

You are flying in an airplane with the wind blowing sharply in your face. You are traveling from Chicago to Nashville. In what direction are you traveling?

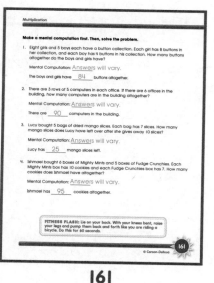

If you said "south" to the above question, you are correct!

Write the direction you would be traveling for each set of cities. Use the four cardinal directions—north, south, east and west.

Atlanta to Los Angeles	west	Houston to Minneapolis __north__
Seattle to Los Angeles	south	Miami to New York __north__
San Francisco to Nashville	east	Detroit to New York __east__
Denver to Salt Lake City	west	Boston to Minneapolis __west__
Cincinnati to Detroit	north	Atlanta to Albuquerque __west__
Chicago to Boston	east	Nashville to Miami __south/east__

164

Answer Key

Page 166

Circle equal groups to find the quotient for each picture.

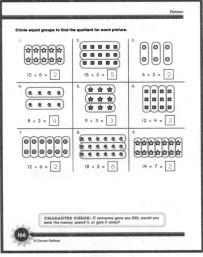

1. $10 \div 5 = \boxed{2}$
2. $15 \div 3 = \boxed{5}$
3. $6 \div 3 = \boxed{2}$
4. $8 \div 2 = \boxed{4}$
5. $9 \div 3 = \boxed{3}$
6. $12 \div 4 = \boxed{3}$
7. $12 \div 6 = \boxed{2}$
8. $18 \div 3 = \boxed{6}$
9. $14 \div 7 = \boxed{2}$

CHARACTER CHECK: If someone gave you $20, would you save the money, spend it, or give it away?

166

Page 167

An exclamatory sentence shows strong emotions or feelings. Write **E** for each exclamatory sentence. Write **D** for each declarative sentence. Write **I** for each interrogative sentence.

1. __I__ What did he do?
2. __E__ I am so happy for you!
3. __E__ It's a girl!
4. __E__ That is terrible news!
5. __D__ The bird is red.
6. __I__ Can I borrow a crayon?

Write each exclamatory sentence with a capital letter and an exclamation point (!).

7. look out __Look out!__
8. i had an amazing day __I had an amazing day!__

Write the missing comparative adjectives.

9. slow __slower__ __slowest__
10. __tall__ taller tallest
11. __warm__ warmer __warmest__
12. bright __brighter__ brightest
13. high __higher__ __highest__
14. kind __kinder__ __kindest__

167

Page 169

Use the passage to answer the questions.

1. If something can be proven or observed, it is a fact. If something can't be proven or observed, it is an opinion. Circle F for fact or O for opinion.

   The animals flew over France for eight minutes. (F) O
   A hot air balloon is so simple, anyone can fly one. F (O)
   It is safer than ever to travel by hot air balloon. (F) O

2. You can often guess what a word means by looking at the words around it. Review the passage and circle each correct answer.

   In the fourth paragraph, the word *sink* means
   (A) to go toward the ground.
   B. to rise up slowly.
   C. a place to wash your hands.

   The word *inflate* means
   A. a new idea.
   (B) to fill something with air.
   C. a safety change.

3. A compound subject is two or more subjects that go with the same verb. Underline the compound subject in each sentence.

   The king of France and two brothers made it happen.
   A major in the army and a physics professor went up.
   Ed Yost and Raven Industries began to design hot air balloons.
   Ed Yost and the Navy made important changes.

4. Irregular verbs do not add *-ed* to make the past tense. They change their form. Write the present tense of each bold verb.

   The king of France **thought** a man would die up in a balloon. __thinks__
   So, two brothers **did** a test. __do__
   Ed Yost and Raven Industries **began** to design hot air balloons. __begin__
   He **sold** hot air balloons for sports events. __sells__

169

Page 170

Complete the following. The first one is done for you.

1. 20 As in all.
   __4__ As in each group.
   How many groups?
   $20 \div 4 = $ __5__
   There are __5__ groups.
   Check: __4 x 5 = 20__

2. 20 As in all.
   __5__ groups of As.
   How many in each group?
   $20 \div 5 = $ __4__
   There are __4__ As in each group.
   Check: __5 x 4 = 20__

3. 12 ☐ in all.
   3 ☐ in each group.
   How many groups?
   $12 \div 4 = $ __4__
   There are __4__ groups.
   Check: __3 x 4 = 12__

4. 12 ☐ in all.
   4 groups of ☐.
   How many in each group?
   $12 \div 4 = $ __3__
   There are __3__ ☐ in each group.
   Check: __4 x 3 = 12__

5. __12__ Fs in all.
   __2__ Fs in each group.
   How many groups?
   $12 \div 2 = $ __6__
   There are __6__ groups.
   Check: __2 x 6 = 12__

6. __12__ Fs in all.
   __6__ groups of Fs.
   How many in each group?
   $12 \div 6 = $ __2__
   There are __2__ Fs in each group.
   Check: __6 x 2 = 12__

FACTOID: It's almost impossible to tickle yourself. Try it!

170

Page 171

Solve each problem.

1. Isabella wants to watch a show at 8:00 p.m. It is 7:23 p.m. How many more minutes is it until the show starts?

   37 minutes

2. Cade's favorite show starts at 7:30 p.m. It is 90 minutes long. What time will the show end?

   9:00 p.m.

3. Taylor's favorite show started at 4:30 p.m. It is 30 minutes long. It is 4:53 p.m. right now. How many more minutes is the show on?

   7 minutes

4. Melissa watched a movie that started at 7:00 p.m. It lasted 1 hour and 47 minutes. What time did the movie end?

   8:47 p.m.

5. Jonathan started watching a show at 4:16 p.m. He turned the television off at 5:37 p.m. How long did he watch television?

   1 hour and 21 minutes

6. Chelsea watched 2 30-minute shows on Monday, 1 30-minute show on Wednesday, and 3 30-minute shows on Friday. How many hours of television did she watch that week?

   3 hours

CHARACTER CHECK: List five ways you can show caring to your friends and family members.

171

Page 172

Write two exclamatory sentences and two declarative sentences. Use a word from the word bank in each sentence.

| attention | calmly | important | free | thousand |
| moment | snow | shiver | station | weird |

1. ___
2. ___
3. ___ Answers will vary.
4. ___

Where is the most exciting place you have ever been? Is it near where you live or far away? Describe this place. What makes it so exciting?

Answers will vary.

172

Answer Key

Page 173

Divide to solve each problem. Draw pictures to help you.
Drawings may vary.

1. $9 \div 3 = 3$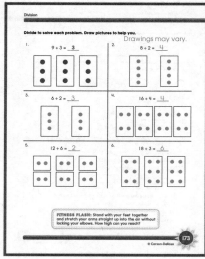
2. $8 \div 2 = 4$
3. $6 \div 2 = 3$
4. $16 \div 4 = 4$
5. $12 \div 6 = 2$
6. $18 \div 3 = 6$

FITNESS FLASH: Stand with your feet together and stretch your arms straight up into the air without locking your elbows. How high can you reach?

173

Page 174

Use the dictionary entry to answer the questions.

gem \'jem\ *n* **1.** jewel **2.** A beloved or prized person or possession

1. What part of speech is *gem*? noun
2. Which definition of *gem* deals with precious stones? 1
3. Would *gemstone* come before or after *gem* in the dictionary? after
4. Use *gem* in a sentence. Answers will vary.

Write a title for each list. Answers may vary.

5. **Birds**
sparrow
wren
blue jay
parrot

6. **Art Supplies**
paper
paste
scissors
markers

7. **Animals**
lion
rhino
bear
hippo

8. **Drinks**
milk
coffee
water
soda

9. **Breakfast Foods**
eggs
toast
bagels
bacon

10. **Insects**
fly
bee
wasp
ant

174

Page 175

Use a ruler to measure each object in centimeters. Then, measure again to the nearest inch.

1. 5 centimeters   about 2 inches
2. 2 centimeters   about 1 inch
3. 13 centimeters   about 5 inches
4. 10 centimeters   about 4 inches
5. 8 centimeters   about 3 inches
6. 16 centimeters   about 6 inches

7. What do you notice about the measurements in centimeters compared to those in inches? The numbers are at least twice as high.

8. What explains this? There are more than 2 centimeters in an inch.

175

Page 177

Use the story to answer the questions.

1. Why were the man and the woman sad at the beginning of the story?
   A. because they were growing old
   B. because they had no children
   C. because the winter was too cold

2. What brought the snow child to life?
   A. a fairy godmother
   B. a snowflake
   C. the woman's kiss

3. The ending *-er* often means "more." Sometimes, it is used to compare two things. The ending *-est* means "most." It is used to compare more than two things. Write a comparative word to complete each sentence. Answers will vary.
   The days are getting warmer now that summer is here.
   That clown looks happier than the one with the frown on his face.
   Jessie's hair is darker than Claudia's.
   Ilene is three years younger than Kevin.
   That statue is higher on the shelf than I thought.

4. Write the base word for each word.
   warmer warm   shorter short
   happier happy   older old

5. Why would the snow child disappear in the spring?
   because she melted with the warm weather

6. In the story, what are some signs of spring?
   • Storms turned to spring showers.
   • The sun began to warm the earth.

7. In the story, what are some signs of winter?
   • The days became shorter and the nights longer.
   • The air was crisp and cool again.

177

Page 178

Divide to solve each problem.

1. Kyle's fish store has 21 goldfish. The fish are in 3 aquariums. The same number of goldfish are in each aquarium. How many goldfish are in each aquarium?
   There are 21 goldfish.
   There are 3 aquariums.
   There are 7 goldfish in each aquarium.

2. Tia has 18 shoes in her closet. A pair of shoes is a group of 2 shoes. How many pairs of shoes does Tia have?
   Tia has 18 shoes.
   A pair is a group of 2 shoes.
   Tia has 9 pairs of shoes.

3. The egg carton has 12 eggs in it. There are 2 rows in the carton. How many eggs are in each row?
   The egg carton has 12 eggs.
   There are 2 rows in the carton.
   There are 6 eggs in each row.

4. Fiona has 16 sticks of gum. If she gives each of her 4 friends the same number of sticks of gum, how many sticks of gum will each of Fiona's friends have?
   Each of Fiona's friends will have 4 sticks of gum.

5. Ben earned 36 dollars for mowing 3 lawns on Saturday. Ben earned the same amount of money for each lawn. How much did he earn for each lawn?
   Ben earned 12 dollars for each lawn he mowed.

178

Page 179

Find the area of each shape.

1. 4 m × 3 m   A = 12 sq. m
2. 7 m × 4 m   A = 28 sq. m
3. 3 m × 8 in.   A = 24 sq. in.
4. 2 cm × 5 cm   A = 10 sq. cm
5. 7 cm × 1 cm   A = 7 sq. cm
6. 4 in. × 3 in.   A = 12 sq. in.

179

Answer Key

A *simple sentence* has one subject and one verb. A *compound sentence* is two simple sentences joined with a conjunction like *and*. A *complex sentence* is a simple sentence combined with a group of words called a *dependent clause*. A dependent clause has a subject and a verb but is not a complete thought.

Read each sentence below. On the line, write *S* if it is a simple sentence, *C* if it is a compound sentence, and *CX* if it is a complex sentence.

1. __C__ The goldfinch ate from the birdfeeder, and then it flew away.
2. __S__ Brian went to the park on Sunday.
3. __CX__ Because Madeline has a beautiful voice, she's going to take singing lessons this fall.
4. __S__ Felicia plays soccer every day.
5. __CX__ Although the temperature dropped last night, the plants were okay.
6. __C__ Derek stopped at the library, but the book he ordered wasn't in yet.

Imagine that when you go to your mailbox one day, you find a treasure map with a letter addressed to you. Write a story about the letter and map. Who sent the letter? If you look for the treasure, do you find it? If you find it, what is it?

Answers will vary.

180

Divide to solve each problem.

1. Rusty wants to save 72 dollars. How many weeks will it take Rusty to save 72 dollars if he saves 9 dollars each week?

   Rusty wants to save __72__ dollars.

   He saves __9__ dollars each week.

   It will take Rusty __8__ weeks to save 72 dollars.

2. Ms. Katz worked 40 hours this week. She worked 8 hours each day. How many days did she work this week?

   Ms. Katz worked __40__ hours this week.

   She worked __8__ hours each day.

   She worked __5__ days this week.

3. There are 22 football players on the field. If there are 11 players on each team, how many teams are on the field?

   There are __22__ football players on the field.

   There are __11__ players on each team.

   There are __2__ teams on the field.

4. Ms. Edwards ordered 66 chairs and 11 tables for a banquet. Each table will have the same number of chairs. How many chairs will be at each table?

   There will be __6__ chairs at each table.

181

Use the story to answer the questions.

1. An idiom is a phrase that means something different from the words that make it up. List three idioms you find in the story on page 182.

   __out of the blue__   Answers may vary.
   __Put a sock in it!__
   __kept their eyes peeled__

2. Write the matching word from the story for each meaning in the word bank.

   | antsy | little |
   | skin | lollygag |

   small __little__   anxious __antsy__

   the outer covering on a body __skin__   to loaf or do nothing __lollygag__

3. Write your own verse for the song "The Ants Go Marching." To keep the rhythm of the song, follow the pattern of the words in the verse on page 182.

   Answers will vary.

4. Predict what might happen next in the story. Write your own ending to the chapter.

   Answers will vary.

183

Fill in the missing numerals to show equivalent fractions.

1. $\frac{1}{3} = \frac{2}{6} = \frac{3}{9} = \frac{4}{12} = \frac{5}{15}$

2. $\frac{1}{4} = \frac{2}{8} = \frac{3}{12} = \frac{4}{16} = \frac{5}{20}$

3. $\frac{2}{3} = \frac{4}{6} = \frac{6}{9} = \frac{8}{12} = \frac{10}{15}$

4. $\frac{3}{4} = \frac{6}{8} = \frac{9}{12} = \frac{12}{16} = \frac{15}{20}$

5. $\frac{4}{5} = \frac{8}{10}$ 6. $\frac{3}{7} = \frac{9}{21}$ 7. $\frac{4}{7} = \frac{16}{28}$ 8. $\frac{3}{4} = \frac{21}{28}$

9. $\frac{7}{8} = \frac{14}{16}$ 10. $\frac{5}{6} = \frac{15}{18}$ 11. $\frac{2}{7} = \frac{12}{42}$ 12. $\frac{2}{5} = \frac{8}{20}$

190

Underline the pronoun that completes each sentence.

1. Dorian borrowed five books from the library, but he has lost one of (it, them).
2. At the fair, several kids lost (them, their) balloons.
3. Uri has two snakes as pets and loves (their, them) very much.
4. Javier remembered to floss (their, his) teeth before bed.
5. The hurricane made landfall at 3:00, and (it, them) is headed this way!
6. Each of the boys gets a sandwich for (her, his) lunch.

Capitalize the first, last, and all important words in a story or book title. Write each story title correctly.
EXAMPLE:

an exciting summer vacation ___An Exciting Summer Vacation___

7. my ride on a horse ___My Ride on a Horse___
8. the day I missed school ___The Day I Missed School___
9. fun, fabulous pets ___Fun, Fabulous Pets___
10. a tornado drill ___A Tornado Drill___
11. my summer project ___My Summer Project___

FACTOID: Oceans cover more than 70 percent of Earth's surface.

191

Divide to solve the problems.

1. $4\overline{)24} = 6$ 2. $4\overline{)16} = 4$ 3. $7\overline{)21} = 3$ 4. $9\overline{)81} = 9$ 5. $6\overline{)18} = 3$

6. $6\overline{)54} = 9$ 7. $9\overline{)27} = 3$ 8. $5\overline{)55} = 11$ 9. $6\overline{)42} = 7$ 10. $5\overline{)5} = 1$

11. $3\overline{)24} = 8$ 12. $4\overline{)28} = 7$ 13. $9\overline{)36} = 4$ 14. $2\overline{)14} = 7$ 15. $1\overline{)9} = 9$

16. $3\overline{)6} = 2$ 17. $9\overline{)18} = 2$ 18. $7\overline{)35} = 5$ 19. $5\overline{)15} = 3$ 20. $3\overline{)9} = 3$

21. $7\overline{)42} = 6$ 22. $9\overline{)45} = 5$ 23. $4\overline{)4} = 1$ 24. $9\overline{)63} = 7$ 25. $2\overline{)6} = 3$

26. $5\overline{)20} = 4$ 27. $2\overline{)18} = 9$ 28. $4\overline{)36} = 9$ 29. $6\overline{)24} = 4$ 30. $8\overline{)72} = 9$

31. $6\overline{)6} = 1$ 32. $8\overline{)64} = 8$ 33. $6\overline{)36} = 6$ 34. $9\overline{)45} = 5$ 35. $3\overline{)18} = 6$

192

Answer Key

193

Use the dictionary entries below to find the answers.

1. Which definition best fits the word *cry* as it is used in this sentence?

   The little girl cried out for her mother.

   Definition number __2__

2. List other forms of the word *cute*. __cuter__ __cutest__

3. Which part of speech is the word *cream*? __noun__

4. Which definition best fits the word *crook* as it is used in this sentence?

   The crook stole the diamond from the museum.

   Definition number __3__

5. What is the definition of the word *dark*?
   __having little or no light__

cream (noun)
1. the yellowish white part of milk

crook (noun)
I carry my umbrella in the crook of my arm.
1. a bent part; curve
2. a shepherd's staff with a hook at the top
3. a person who is not honest

cry (verb)
1. to shed tears; weep.
The hungry baby cried.
2. to call out loudly; shout.
The people in the burning building were crying for help.

cute (adjective)
1. delightful or pretty.
This is the cutest puppy I have ever seen.

dark (adjective)
1. having little or no light
The night was dark because the clouds covered the moon.

dash (verb)
1. to move fast; rush
We dashed to the waiting bus.
2. to destroy or ruin
Spraining my ankle dashed my hopes of running in the race.

194

Complete each sentence. Circle the measurement that makes the most sense.

1. My Dad is _____ tall. 6 inches (6 feet)

2. My math book is _____ wide. (9 inches) 9 feet

3. My big toe is _____ long. (1 inch) 1 foot

4. My new baby sister is _____ long. (20 inches) 20 feet

Measure the shape at the right with a ruler.

5. What is the length of the rectangle? __2__ in.

6. What is the width of the rectangle? __1__ in.

7. Add the measurements of the 4 sides of the rectangle to find its perimeter.

   __2__ inches + __2__ inches + __1__ inches + __1__ inches = __6__ inches

195

Underline an adverb to complete each sentence.

1. Our puppy plays (more happily, happier) with children than with anyone else.

2. Jorge arrived (latest, most late) to class.

3. Please try to whisper (softer, more softly) while the baby sleeps.

4. Forrest jumped (most high, highest) of anyone in the competition.

5. The stars seem to shine (brightliest, most brightly) far from the city.

6. My brother completed the activity (carefullier, more carefully) than I did.

Similar words can have different shades of meaning. Write each word in the sentence where it makes the most sense.

7. **happy, overjoyed**

   Shannon was __overjoyed__ to see her grandparents for the first time in nearly ten years.

   Paul was __happy__ that he could sleep in on Saturday morning.

8. **upset, outraged**

   Pedro felt __upset__ when he couldn't find his soccer cleats.

   Mrs. Kwan was __outraged__ that the babysitter forgot to pick up the kids at school.

9. **gigantic, large**

   A __large__ moth fluttered around the porch light.

   During the tsunami, several __gigantic__ waves nearly destroyed the village.

196

Find the area of each shape.

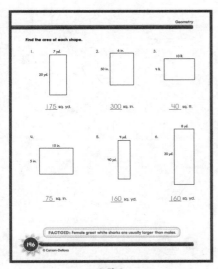

1. 7 yd. × 25 yd. __175__ sq. yd.

2. 6 in. × 50 in. __300__ sq. in.

3. 10 ft. × 4 ft. __40__ sq. ft.

4. 15 in. × 5 in. __75__ sq. in.

5. 4 yd. × 40 yd. __160__ sq. yd.

6. 8 yd. × 20 yd. __160__ sq. yd.

FACTOID: Female great white sharks are usually larger than males.

197

Your teacher asks you to write a report about animals. In the report, you must answer all of the questions listed below. It would take a very long time to read the entire book, so you decide to use the table of contents to help you. Write the chapter and page number where you would look to answer each question.

Table of Contents		
Chapter 1	Mammals (Animals with Fur)	3
Chapter 2	Reptiles (Snakes and Turtles)	13
Chapter 3	Amphibians (Frogs and Toads)	21
Chapter 4	Fish	35
Chapter 5	Insects and Spiders	49
Chapter 6	Birds	57

	Chapter	Page
1. How long do lions live?	1	3
2. How fast do sailfish swim?	4	35
3. What do snakes eat?	2	13
4. How long does it take for robin eggs to hatch?	6	57
5. Do spiders bite?	5	49
6. Where do poison dart frogs live?	3	21
7. What do beavers eat?	1	3
8. How long do turtles live?	2	13

198

Use the missing factor to help you find the quotient.

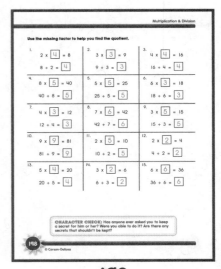

1. $2 \times 4 = 8$ $8 \div 2 = 4$
2. $3 \times 3 = 9$ $9 \div 3 = 3$
3. $4 \times 4 = 16$ $16 \div 4 = 4$
4. $8 \times 5 = 40$ $40 \div 8 = 5$
5. $5 \times 5 = 25$ $25 \div 5 = 5$
6. $6 \times 3 = 18$ $18 \div 6 = 3$
7. $4 \times 3 = 12$ $12 \div 4 = 3$
8. $7 \times 6 = 42$ $42 \div 7 = 6$
9. $3 \times 5 = 15$ $15 \div 3 = 5$
10. $9 \times 9 = 81$ $81 \div 9 = 9$
11. $2 \times 5 = 10$ $10 \div 2 = 5$
12. $2 \times 2 = 4$ $4 \div 2 = 2$
13. $5 \times 4 = 20$ $20 \div 5 = 4$
14. $3 \times 2 = 6$ $6 \div 3 = 2$
15. $6 \times 6 = 36$ $36 \div 6 = 6$

CHARACTER CHECK: Has anyone ever asked you to keep a secret for him or her? Were you able to do it? Are there any secrets that shouldn't be kept?

Answer Key

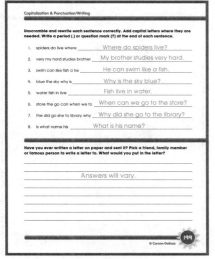

199

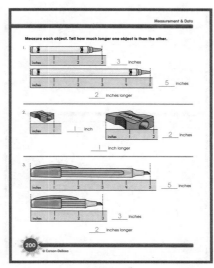

200

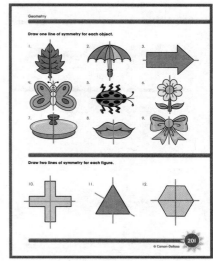

201

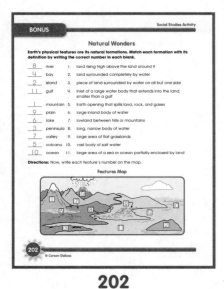

202

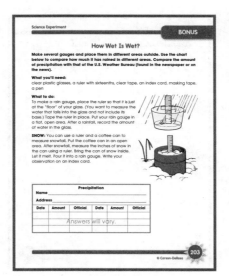

203

204

243

© Carson-Dellosa

Answer Key

Circle each correct answer.

1. A wading pool holds about: 500 grams 500 liters (5,000 liters)
2. A refrigerator weighs about: 90 grams (90 kilograms) 9 kilograms
3. A nail weighs about: (1 gram) 100 grams 1,000 grams
4. A small dog weighs about: 15 grams 50 grams (5,000 grams)

Solve using addition and subtraction.

5. Warren brought 4 quarts of milk for the party. Ian brought 6 quarts of milk for the party. How many more quarts of milk did Ian bring than Warren?

   Ian brought __2__ more quarts of milk than Warren.

6. Delaina's bag of fruit weighs 32 ounces. Ken's bag of fruit weighs 14 ounces. How many ounces do Delaina and Ken's bags weigh altogether?

   Delaina and Ken's bags of fruit weigh __46__ ounces altogether.

7. Roberto had 18 gallons of paint to paint his entire house. He only used 11 gallons. How many gallons of paint does Roberto have left?

   Roberto has __7__ gallons of paint left.

8. Jenna weighed 3 kilograms when she was born. Now she weighs 13 kilograms. How much weight did Jenna gain since she was born?

   Jenna gained __10__ kilograms since she was born.

205

Add commas and quotation marks where they are needed. Use this symbol to add a comma ⌄ and this symbol to add quotation marks ⌄.

1. I asked, "Did you know that Renee lives in Billings, Montana?"
2. "Mr. Chu is my neighbor," said Grandpa.
3. "Is Geneva's birthday in May?" asked Isabel.
4. "My mother and I shop at Miller's Market," I added.
5. "What is your favorite day of the week?" asked Wendy.

Add a simple sentence after each conjunction below to form a compound sentence.
EXAMPLE: Mr. Edwards is a teacher, but
Mr. Edwards is a teacher, but I'm not in his class.

Answers will vary.

6. Dad is teaching Sean how to fix the car, but

7. Hayley feeds the dog each morning, or

8. It is supposed to rain on Saturday, so

9. Chrissie just joined the basketball team, and

206

Write two multiplication and two division equations for each fact family.

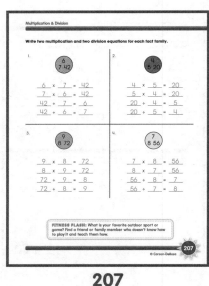

1.
6 7 42
  6 x 7 = 42
  7 x 6 = 42
  42 ÷ 7 = 6
  42 ÷ 6 = 7

2.
4 5 20
  4 x 5 = 20
  5 x 4 = 20
  20 ÷ 4 = 5
  20 ÷ 5 = 4

3.
9 8 72
  9 x 8 = 72
  8 x 9 = 72
  72 ÷ 9 = 8
  72 ÷ 8 = 9

4.
7 8 56
  7 x 8 = 56
  8 x 7 = 56
  56 ÷ 8 = 7
  56 ÷ 7 = 8

FITNESS FLASH: What is your favorite outdoor sport or game? Find a friend or family member who doesn't know how to play it and teach them how.

207

Divide each shape into the given amount of equal parts. Then, label each piece with the appropriate fraction.

Drawings may vary.

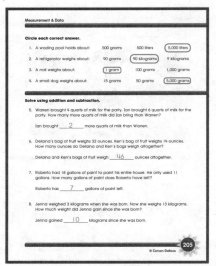

1. thirds
2. halves
3. halves
4. thirds
5. fourths
6. fourths
7. halves
8. fifths
9. halves
10. fifths

208

Write the name of the person who is talking in each sentence.

1. Seth said, "Scott, you need to get out of bed." __Seth__
2. "Is this your video game, Lamonte?" asked Khalil. __Khalil__
3. Lamonte replied, "No, Khalil, it is not my video game." __Lamonte__
4. "Will you take the dog for a walk, Mona?" asked Mrs. Benson. __Mrs. Benson__
5. "Would you please go to the store for me?" Shazia asked. __Shazia__

Rewrite each sentence correctly. Add capital letters, periods, and question marks where they are needed.

6. bridget has a cat named spot
   Bridget has a cat named Spot.

7. do robins eat worms
   Do robins eat worms?

8. can I play with your soccer ball
   Can I play with your soccer ball?

9. my name is neyla
   My name is Neyla.

209

Divide or multiply to solve the problems.

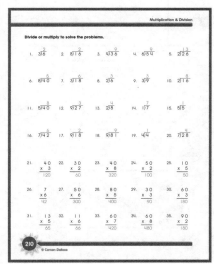
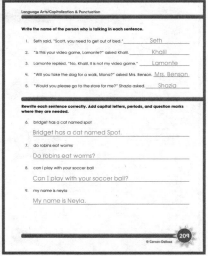

1. 3)6 = 2
2. 8)16 = 2
3. 4)36 = 9
4. 6)54 = 9
5. 2)26 = 13

6. 8)40 = 5
7. 3)18 = 6
8. 2)26 = ...
9. 3)9 = 3
10. 2)16 = 8

11. 5)40 = 8
12. 9)27 = 3
13. 2)8 = 4
14. 1)17 = ...
15. 5)25 = 5

16. 7)42 = 6
17. 2)18 = ...
18. 9)81 = 9
19. 4)16 = 4
20. 2)28 = 14

21. 40 x 3 = 120
22. 30 x 2 = 60
23. 40 x 8 = 320
24. 50 x 2 = 100
25. 10 x 5 = 50

26. 7 x 6 = 42
27. 50 x 6 = 300
28. 80 x 4 = 320
29. 30 x 3 = 90
30. 60 x 3 = 180

31. 13 x 5 = 65
32. 11 x 6 = 66
33. 60 x 7 = 420
34. 60 x 8 = 480
35. 90 x 2 = 180

210

Answer Key

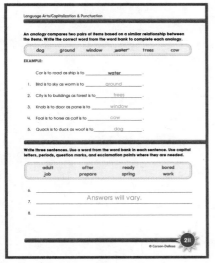

211

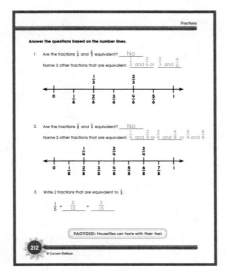

212

216

Notes